BUILDING CRAFT FOREMANSHIP

BUILDING CRAFT FOREMANSHIP

R. HOWARTH
FBICC, FIMWoodT, MISM, LIOB, AIWSc

DAVID & CHARLES: NEWTON ABBOT

0 7153 5667 4

Set in 11 on 13 Times Roman
and printed in Great Britain
by Bristol Typesetting Company Limited
for David & Charles (Publishers) Limited
South Devon House Newton Abbot Devon

To My Wife

Preface

This book has been written in the hope that it will help the potential craft foreman, or the young building tradesman who may aspire to this position, to develop skills and confidence in his ability to fulfil the supervisory tasks which may be assigned to him.

Basically, the contents were designed to meet the requirements of the City & Guilds Full Technological Certificate Course subject of Craft Foremanship Studies, with the coverage arranged under 29 sections (as a teaching breakdown) in the same chronological order as presented in the syllabus.

It is hoped that the book will cover the appropriate requirement of supervision for the FTC course for painters and decorators work, and for the following examinations:

Construction Site Organisation, (Supplementary Studies, City & Guilds Subject No 626).

Construction Site Supervision, (City & Guilds Subject No 628).

The subject of Professional Practice and Procedure, for the final Examination of the Institute of Clerk of Works.

The contents should also cover the basic principles of supervisory work in building for students taking Supervisory Courses in Construction, or building employees taking the National Examinations Board Certificate in Supervisory Studies.

R.H.

Acknowledgements

I wish to acknowledge my grateful thanks for the help and co-operation of the following firms and organisations for allowing me to use information, illustrations and material in the text: The Controller of Her Majesty's Stationery Office (illustrations); The National Joint Council for the Building Industry (text); The Royal Institute of British Architects (text); The National Federation of Building Trade Employers (charts and text); The Federation of Master Builders (text); Rank Precision Industries Limited, Metrology Division; Hilger and Watts Limited (surveying and levelling instruments); G. P. Services (Western) Limited (Quick-Sight Level).

I am also indebted to my good friend, J. Pugh, AIOB, for his advice and help in preparing the example on Quantities; to C. Haywood, AIOB, the City & Guilds Chief Examiner in this subject, for reading the script and offering constructive suggestions for publication; and to my wife, for her constant encouragement.

Contents

List of Charts, Forms and Illustrations

PART ONE

ELEMENTS OF CRAFT LEADERSHIP

1

Qualities and Qualifications

The building industry is fast becoming very complex. Pre-fabricated and industrialised methods of construction and the use of new materials have brought about completely new ideas of supervision. Speedier building with smaller labour forces has demanded a more scientific approach to the building team and its forms of management, resulting in an endeavour to select and train its supervisory staff.

The fear of unemployment, and the shadow of the hawk-eyed, bowler-hatted, burly, bully of a foreman has now disappeared from the industry. Today, with better general working conditions and an apprenticeship scheme, the trade offers better prospects and a good promotion ladder for the keen and energetic entrant.

Although much has been done through the spread of further education and the various courses and examinations which have resulted, there is still a shortage of properly selected and trained supervisors in the industry.

Firms are now beginning to realise that tradition has no part in good leadership, and that they must play a part in the responsibility of training supervisory staff. Already the vision of the Industrial Training Act of 1964 is beginning to materialise with the comprehensive scheme of training, but much has still to be done and it is the duty of all firms to participate in this selection and training of leaders in the full interests of the industry.

TYPE OF CANDIDATE

Many people believe that leaders are born, and many employers believe super craftsmen make the best foremen, but neither of these characteristics is essentially true, nor can one use these general inferences.

While it is true that some individuals are capable, or competent, of obtaining the co-operation of others without much effort, there are also others whose personal qualities could be improved by good training.

PERSONAL QUALITIES

Essentially the foreman should have the desire to be a leader. He must be fit and have physical vitality or energy; be loyal both to his employer and his fellows, and possess self-confidence, which can be passed to others. Honesty of character, sound morals, and personal integrity are essential and he must be patient, understanding, unselfish, and have a sense of humour.

Perhaps conservative in dress, but outstanding and smart in appearance, he will have a good personality, and be able to get on with others. He must express himself clearly, and exercise discipline, having the ability to plan and organise. Truthful, tidy, and tactful, he will have respect for workers, and a willingness to give credit, with an ability to sense annoyance and disputes. He must be straightforward, and able to demonstrate justice; be concise and to the point. He will never show off his ability, or take advantage of his position.

The foreman's place in management He must know the policy of his firm and be acquainted with the likely developments so that he can play his part. He should be familiar with the firm's office routine, and be taken into confidence with certain legal, finance and accounting routines. He must be given the responsibility for supervision and direction of labour.

The foreman as a manager of men He should assign operatives to their jobs, and encourage operatives to better work or production. He must co-ordinate the effort of all workmen under his control, always interpret the firm's policy, and maintain fair and impartial supervision. To maintain good working conditions, he will keep good discipline and time-keeping, and try to settle all disputes and complaints.

TECHNICAL QUALIFICATIONS

The potential foreman should have served an apprenticeship and be competent in his craft. He must possess a City & Guilds certificate in his craft (which to some degree would certify his competence). But one must be flexible on this score, as many first class men could by experience have leadership qualities. As site management in the future is likely to be more dependent on training, initial craft qualifications would suggest potential for the training ladder.

Irrespective of qualifications, the prospective foreman should be able to communicate effectively in the spoken and written word. Technical qualifications are much more in demand for posts, as greater responsibility demands a wider knowledge. Qualifications and experience ultimately lead to professional status for the foreman who hopes to aspire to the ranks of general foreman, agent, or clerk of works.

FOREMAN'S DAILY DUTIES

Receive instructions and study all given documents.
See that instructions and requirements are carried out.
Plan progress and time and progress schedules.
Plan the preparation of transport, tools, materials, plant, and storage.
Try to have good relations, respect and confidence.
Consider the requirements of sub-contractors.
Set standards of quality and targets.
Order materials, and ensure adequate supply.

Notify and give access of plant and 'attendance' to sub-contractors.

Be efficient and tactful in the management of men.

Be conversant with industrial, trade, and other new information or regulations and news.

Praise men and encourage them with performances.

Instruct and train apprentices and trainees, and try to win confidence.

Maintain good working conditions and amenities.

Be rational, and establish a fair system of supervision.

Be fair in any disputes or breakdown of plans.

Make suggestions to improve methods in the use of men, materials, space or time.

Interpret the firm's policy, but be prepared to receive complaints.

Where necessary, recommend promotion or rate increases.

Co-ordinate the work of all under his control.

Keep necessary records of the job and its progress.

Check on quantities, extras, and variations.

Check all setting out and levels.

Gain permits, or any permission required.

Give necessary notices to local authority.

Inform sub-contractors of necessary work, requirements, or any alterations in plans or contract.

2

The Team Spirit

In order that the foreman might cultivate team spirit and realise the situations where discipline may be required, it is important that he could understand something of human nature.

THE PSYCHOLOGICAL MAKE-UP OF MEN

It is held that workmen are lazy, hate supervision, try to avoid work, have no regard for their fellow men and only strive after luxury. It has, however, been shown from investigations that men are products of circumstance, and that changes in conditions around them can have remarkable results.

It may help the foreman in his understanding of his men, and aim to develop teamwork, to know that scientific investigations have determined that the 'essential desires of men at work' (in order of importance) are: regularity and security of employment; high standard of net wages; reasonable hours of work; considerate supervision; comfortable working conditions; congenial and interesting work; acceptable workmates; possibilities of promotion; and limited personal responsibility.

Team spirit has been defined as, 'the continuous condition of working together which makes the most of the circumstances, equipment, and persons, both individually and collectively in the common interest of all.' *The team spirit in building* depends upon the ability of the foreman to lead, as workmen have a right to expect efficient leadership if they are to give of their best.

Cultivation of team spirit is not easy and demands much to achieve success; it is difficult because human beings are influenced by feelings, ambitions, and their personal likes and dislikes.

To achieve team spirit it is important to understand what makes the operatives want to work. They work to earn a living, and to receive a fair day's pay for a fair day's work; for the possibility of advancement or promotion and pride in the work, or appreciation of the craft.

Team spirit will not exist where there is no understanding of the firm's policy, or a lack of information or proper instructions; a failure to train others or delegate responsibility; a lack of discipline or firmness; allowing friction or the disregard of authority to develop; lack of confidence or co-operation.

How the foreman can create team spirit: Do not let pressure of work prevent mixing with the men and maintain good working conditions. Present the goal and ultmate target to the workers. Always be proud of the task or job (but not boastful).

Tackle every job with enthusiasm, as this is contagious, always appear to be busy or working, and enlist interest from charge hands. Try to plan work so that one operation at a time can be completed, so that some degree of progress can be seen. Be fair and considerate to all under your control.

The foreman can only get full team spirit with the co-operation of all the men. The men will respond only in proportion to the amount of team spirit, leadership, and enthusiasm, seen to be emitted by the foreman.

Where team spirit exists: the workman knows that he will get a square deal from his foreman. The operative knows that credit will be given where it is due, and suggestions will be considered. The men will require less supervision and there will be less site troubles or grievances. As better working conditions will ensue, the workmen are likely to think more of their jobs with greater pride and better results.

Where team spirit is lacking not only will there be irresponsibility and dissatisfaction, but the lack of leadership will also reflect in errors and mistakes which result in wastage. Teamwork demands that every worker will have a role to play, and where this is lacking targets and standards will fail to be reached. Where incentives and bonus schemes are in operation there will be discontent and criticism of management downwards will become the order of the day.

DISCIPLINE

Discipline means orderly conduct, and it is essential in any group effort of employment; without some form of discipline a day's pay would never be earned, or a day's planned work completed. In the present building industry, we have lost the old threat of dismissal in order to maintain discipline. The modern foreman needs the support, interest, and suggestions, from his labour force and these will only be achieved by leadership and co-operation, not by fear.

Situations requiring discipline: (i) Bad time-keeping. (ii) Poor workmanship. (iii) Theft. (iv) Waste of materials. (v) Insubordination. (vi) Carelessness to safety. (vii) Ill-treatment of plant, machines etc.

Limitations and applications of discipline: (i) instant dismissal or the serving of notice, (ii) a reprimand, or threat of dismissal on re-occurrence, (iii) loss of bonus or incentive, (where employed) if bad workmanship has been carried out, (iv) loss of wage for time lost through bad time-keeping.

The foreman's action before dismissal: Every foreman is

faced at some time or other with the perplexing and unpleasant task of reducing his labour force. In case of redundancy, give reasonable advance notice

For disciplinary action, use discharge or dismissal sparingly, as few actions rarely fully deserve the sack.

Decisions in discipline: the foreman must realise that discipline will not be necessary if every worker is fully informed as to what he can do, and what he cannot do. Conscience coupled with experience should tell the worker how far he can go, but the example of the foreman should be a final guide. Before making any decisions concerning discipline, the foreman should base his actions on facts, get all the facts and never rely on second-hand information. Never jump to conclusions because of a worker's past, or past incidents. Do not assume that dismissal over one error will stop others making that error, it may have originated through a lack of supervision or instructions. Never assume that dismissal will act as a threat to others or create better support, it may have the reverse effect. When in doubt as to a decision in discipline, base the decision on a factual case, which can leave no doubt as to its justice.

Maintaining discipline: discipline is a means to an end rather than an achievement in itself, and its purpose is to promote good conduct within the working group. Discipline should be constructive and persuasive rather than destructive and aggressive. Measures adopted should encourage better work rather than the possibility of any resentment or criticism. Any action taken should fit the crime, so that the culprit will appreciate his error.

To maintain discipline, the foreman must exercise continuous and consistent supervision. He must not make his own rules or break any in order to exercise justice over others.

A good disciplinarian is one who finds all the facts before taking action; is calm, cool, and collected, and not easily provoked; is consistent in his actions and decisions; is firm yet fair, and imperturbable; is considerate and tactful in his dealings; is able to set a good example, and gain respect from the men; and is not prejudiced or gives prejudgment.

HOW TO CORRECT WORKERS

Get all the facts and ensure that they are genuine. Be fair and considerate when weighing up the facts. Any conclusions must be as sound as the facts upon which those conclusions are based.

Check the operative's reasons by putting yourself in the workers' place, and trying to discover his motive. Assess reasons for the operative's mistakes or failings, and ensure that you were not to blame or lacking, and that this led to the initial failing.

Choose proper correction by considering all the facts, and the worker's reasons, excuses, or alibi, before you decide on a course of action to take. Be sure that your action is right, and that the punishment fits the crime.

When correcting the worker, indicate that you wish to be helpful. Be tolerant, tactful, patient, and be prepared to accept the worker's word to improve once he has been corrected. This confidence can do much to improve the worker's impression of you. Always conduct your disciplinary actions or correcting in private.

Constructive approach to correcting workers: to prevent any repetition of failure instead of trying to correct the mistake; to try and correct permanently instead of creating a temporary solution; to remedy the faults rather than condemn the operative, and to try to improve standards and force production instead of intimidating the workers.

Causes of dismissal. The foreman may be interested, and he might gain guidance from statistics on some research on the cause of dismissal, carried out by Dr Brewer, of Harvard

University. Out of a sample of some 4,174 test cases, 62.4 per cent of those dismissed involved personal characteristics like insubordination, absenteeism, and unreliability; while lack of skills accounted for 34.2 per cent. Other causes and percentages involved were:—

Carelessness	14%	Lack of Initiative	7%
Non-co-operation	10%	Lateness	7%
Laziness	10%	Lack of Effort	7%
Dishonesty	8%	Disloyalty	3%
Attention to other		Discourtesy	2%
interests	8%	Miscellaneous	24%

Effect of the Working Rule Agreement Where the worker finds safeguards and security, it would be reasonable to suggest that team spirit will improve, and many disciplinary troubles will be minimised.

Certain safeguards and security in the way of the following working conditions are provided for in the National Working Rules, under the terms of settlement of 17 December 1969:

(1) Standard rates of wages to be expressed as weekly amounts.
(2) Guaranteed weekly wage.
(3) Extension of incentive schemes and productivity agreements.
(4) Qualifying period for entitlement to annual and public holiday credit stamps.
(5) Revised disputes procedures.

3

Good Workmanship

PLANNING AND CONTROL

Apart from giving quality and enhancing the reputation of the firm, good workmanship produces a sense of satisfaction to the worker resulting in less supervision for the foreman.

Good workmanship may lead to
Use of better and more expensive materials.
Longer contract in maintaining standards. } Greater Costs
More workers to execute the work.

Costs and the foreman As will be seen above, good workmanship can lead to higher costs, and it is important that the basic elements of costing as they apply to building work is understood by the foreman in order that he can see where greater costs would influence the selling price.

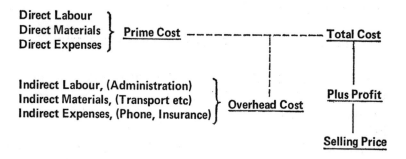

The foreman and cost control If good workmanship is likely to lead to increased costs, and increased prime cost leads to a greater selling price, then some economy is required by some planning and control.

Prime cost increases In order to reveal if the prime cost of any job is to increase, the foreman can make a survey of at least the wastage caused by the labour force:

Do the men arrive and start work on time?
Do they work a full day or finish too soon?
Are the meal and tea breaks abused?
Are there too many operatives retained on the job?
Is overtime being worked unnecessarily?
Are bonus and incentive rates too excessive?
Is there too much waiting time for transport or materials?
Is there too much absenteeism?
Is there time-wasting or slackness?
Are skilled men doing low grade work?
Are men kept waiting for orders or instructions?
Are there delays due to shortage of tools or plant?
Has the working effort really been planned?
Are the men fully trained or briefed for the work they are engaged on?
Do the men know the output or daily standards expected?
Is there a good team spirit and co-operation?
Is the most being made of new ideas and suggestions?
Is the foreman wasting time?

PROMOTION OF GOOD CRAFTSMANSHIP

The craftsman has been described as, 'the worker fulfilling society's or industry's need for a specialist; he is an essential member of society and his vocation or craft is as old as humanity'.

The Old Testament prophet said, 'Without these [craftsmen], cities cannot be built, nor inhabited, nor occupied, they maintain the state of the world and their desire is concerning their work and occupation'.

Perhaps it would be well if not only the foreman, but everyone connected with the building industry occasionally reflected on the above definitions.

Difference between craftsmen and workers There are three distinct characteristics inherent in the craftsman, which make him differ from an ordinary worker; he can marry beauty and utility, and exercise good taste and usefulness with all that is demanded of him; he can produce a complete work and finish without being dependent on complex tools, machinery, or plant; and since 'Nothing in the past is dead to the man who has learned how the present came to be what it is', the craftsman can adapt himself to copy tradition or produce utility.

Although there are many forms of building crafts which differ in the processing, repair, or creative work which they do, most building workers are creative in that in the main they take raw materials and convert them into a finished product.

Whatever form the work or craft takes, the foreman can help to promote good craftsmanship by giving praise and credit for good work done. He can give the worker a sense of individual responsibility and show a particular interest in skill and craftsmanship. Where possible, give incentives of rewards for good work. Encourage participation in group work, where older and experienced craftsmen can give a lead and encourage younger workers. He can promote the working conditions and facilities, which will help workers to give of their best; shun bad work, and recognise differences in skills; and exercise good leadership by fixing good standards and quality.

Good craftsmanship leads to quality, which is characteristic of the finish of a product. Craftsmanship in industry is not the look of perfection, but the degree to which a product conforms to requirements. It is necessary to meet the demands of the customer and satisfy the requirements of construction and regulations. Improved skills and methods will ensure that defects will not occur, and the best advertisement for craftsmanship, is in the production of a building which will give satisfied customers.

Good craftsmanship can improve the firm's reputation on the market; eliminate costs in rectifying poor work; prevent waste or mis-use of materials; minimise the time and cost of supervision and inspection, and prevent complaints from dissatisfied customers.

The foreman's task in promotion He must inspire the pride of good work and the sense of being customer-conscious. He must outline clearly the quality and quantity of work. In respect of quality, he should try to maintain standards and improve on them and carry out careful and regular inspection of work.

QUALITY AND QUANTITY OF WORK

Quality must take priority over quantity, as it is essential to get the required standard of work before the volume can be increased, otherwise there would be too much sub-standard work. Normally, if the quality of work is high, the output will be low, resulting in a higher cost of production. This is a situation where the foreman must consider if the work being done is adding to the value of the job or merely to the costs. To avoid wasting time in attempting to gain quality, the quality should be gained and controlled by fixing standards. Once standards have been decided upon and fixed, the volume of work must then be adjusted to the required level.

Standards of quality can be fixed and measured, it is not a dream or fantasy. The quality of the work must offer reasonable value to the client. Any quality must be such as to meet the requirements and Tests of the Building Regulations, 1965. Standards set for one trade should be similar, as far as trade quality is concerned, to other trades, but quality of work will very often depend on site or working conditions.

In view of the above paragraph the foreman might consider the production or making of components off site. Quality standards of one trade should be sufficient so as not to lower the standard of the work for following trades.

Causes of poor quality work These are the things which the foreman might observe and try to correct:

1. Individual: (i) lack of interest or thoughtlessness of the operatives; (ii) lack of experience, or changing workers where one finishes what another has started; (iii) carelessness allowed to go on without correction; (iv) the operative being completely unsuitable for the type or standard of work; (v) too great an output demanded for the quality required; and (vi) bad supervision, either too much or too little.

2. Information: (i) insufficient or precise instructions not being given; (ii) the standards of quality not being defined; and (iii) inadequate or out-dated methods of construction.

3. Materials: (i) Using wrong or inferior materials; (ii) lack of inspection of materials, either in use or on being received; and (iii) lack of rejection of previous inferior work.

4. Plant, tools, or equipment: (i) antiquated or unsuitable for the work being done; (ii) lack of plant, etc or make-shift substitutes; and (iii) overworked machines, or lack of maintenance.

5. Conditions: (i) an untidy, dirty, or disorderly site or work-place; (ii) lack of welfare provisions, (dampness, light, heat); (iii) bad transport, or poor storage or stacking; (iv) lack of safety precautions; and (v) poor site lay-out, involving congestion of work or materials.

How to improve work quality

1. Determine the standards: (i) consider the job requirements; (ii) consider local or trade practices in view of the above demands; (iii) after the above considerations, decide on

C

the standards and variations both for completed and part-completed work; and (iv) define the standards clearly either in writing, sample, or example, according to Trade.

2. Check the standard: (i) decided how much, and where and when, supervision is required; (ii) check standards fairly and impartially; (iii) define and assign responsibility of the work to individuals; and (iv) during some inspection jobs, (drains, levels, setting-out), assisting personnel can be 'trained' in standard requirements.

3. Prevent wastage: (i) be conversant with the standards and specification of the materials; (ii) where waste occurs, arrange for disposal; (iii) rectify defective work immediately; (iv) wastage in some trades will be dependent on bad storage of materials, or badly maintained tools and plant.

4. How to maintain quality: (i) think, talk, and sell quality all the time; (ii) praise work which is of good quality; (iii) encourage ideas on improving quality; (iv) always inform new workers or sub-contractors of quality requirements; (v) check quality work samples with master samples; and (vi) where incentive schemes are in operation, try to square quality with the bonus given.

When to make inspections Defective work should be discovered as quickly as possible, so as to prevent further work being done on a defective 'foundation'. Inspection should occur at stages of work where failure would be expensive. Inspect any work before there is a concealing operation, such as plastering, painting etc. Inspect work before handing over to other trades or sub-contractors, in order to avoid later disputes over responsibility.

In work like concreting, 'wet trades' or similar jobs, in cold weather, inspect at the beginning of large mixes or batches so that early discovery might prevent extensive waste through frost etc.

PART TWO

SITE AND WORKSHOP ORGANISATION

4

Efficient Control of Craft Force

The purpose of efficient control of any workers is what one hopes to achieve. The effect of efficient control, is the result that one would get.

Efficient control should produce better workmanship or craftsmanship, as well as a better team spirit. It should reduce costs and wastage in labour and materials, and improve the working organisation.

The foreman does not have to be an accountant in order to have some idea of control of costs. If the foreman knows or realises what actions on his part will send the job costs up or down, this is the basic fundamental of cost accounting. The delivery of materials and weather conditions probably have a greater effect on the building industry than any other, and it may be argued that these cannot be controlled, but the foreman can do more about the effects of them than anyone else.

The foreman and costing He can keep down costs by better management, and he must understand that every decision he makes will be reflected in costs. He should have a simple, yet effective, system of keeping cost records, not by compiling figures or maintaining ledgers, but by having some yardstick against which the work or job results can be measured. In planning work, break the jobs down into parts and set objectives in terms of time and costs that you think these actions will take. Experience and time will prove if your parts and objectives are realistic.

How the foreman can reduce labour costs Ensure that every operative fully knows what is expected of him in a day's work. Aim to get a fair day's work from all workers on every job. Keep an eye on the layout of the job and plant and methods used, as these are just as important as the worker's individual efforts.

Do not 'overman' jobs, remember that where incentives are used eight men could be employed on a job which could easily be done by six men, and they could earn a higher bonus. Waiting time for orders, materials, or repairs to machines or plant, are always a total loss. Apart from the direct labour employed, keep an eye on indirect labour and the time wasted on transport, cleaning up, or storekeeping etc. Always insist on fair but accurate time-keeping.

Reducing material costs These are somewhat easier to control than labour costs. Are you getting the greatest yield without waste from the materials used, and can you still further reduce the waste, scrap, or off-cuts? See that operatives understand the value of the materials they are using. It may be worth having an 'exhibition' of materials with price tags on once in a while to press home these facts. The correct protection and handling of materials (see Chapter 8), can concurrently help them to understand material value.

The misuse of power, heat, and light, as well as running taps on metered water can all help to increase costs, even though they do not greatly affect building operations. They do nothing to enhance the reputation of the firm. Give instructions to turn off unwanted lights, power, and machines, and ensure maintenance is carried out to correct the wastage.

Control of the craft force Nothing gets done efficiently without good organisation, which can be summarised as being the promotion of order, routines, arrangements and plans, which will give results. Good organisation will lead to a full investigation of the work and result in method and planning of men, materials, and plant.

Sub-Contract Work Good organisation is essential where specialists or sub-contractors are employed in order that these may work in harmony with the trade concerned. Thus the foreman may be involved in dividing up work into short-cycle operations in order to accommodate the specialist, also to co-ordinate the stages of work so that it is executed as quickly and cheaply as possible.

Good organisation is based on the following:

Harmony, produced by team spirit, good relations, and the avoidance of friction.

Purpose, where proper information and instructions are given.

Planning, correct methods of construction, and the proper use of men, materials, and plant.

Efficiency, correct job balance which will prevent fatigue or monotony of work.

Order, the state of the job in cleanliness or tidiness, will determine if it reflects where organisation prevails.

Progress, allowing for new ideas and methods as well as flexibility.

The foreman should delegate duties and authority to sub-ordinates, and see that all major instructions are carried out. Duties and responsibilities should be clearly defined, so that every worker knows his limitations. Plan the work on the men available, and try to eliminate job movement. Simplify work so that one man performs one job or function. Always be ready to seek or receive ways of improvement, and demonstrate organisation with one's own work or example. Be ready to change a plan, but only after proper preparation. Always think first before acting, remembering that planning and preparation should always come before performance.

5

Deployment of Labour

A planned sequence of operations, and a well deployed labour force, should result in good production control. This means that with proper planning, and a system of prepared progress, the greatest possible use can be made of men, materials, and plant. Work control should prevent wasted time, and allow the foreman to deal more adequately with supervision.

Operation Planning is needed to arrive at an economic date for the completion of the job. This time factor will decide on the number of men and plant requirements. Planning will enable an overall job programme to be made from the decided sequence of operations.

Date for completion of work Consider any restricted time for operations such as week-ends for businesses, eg jobs at shops and cafés when closed. Contract dead line, perhaps with penalty clause. Give consideration of inconvenience to client. Remember pressure of work may prevent movement of men from other jobs, and the time of year may restrict hours of daylight or the working of overtime. Consider public holidays and the annual holidays of the client or workers.

If the job is small, after considering the time factor, make a forecast of men and possible plant, and a planning of sequence of operations.

Considerations if large job or site work The distance from the firm's headquarters to site; site lay-out and accommodation; type of ground, if excavation has to be carried out; any existing services, drains, water, electricity; scope of contract, and any conditions; the position of labour, and if any work should be sub-let; the possibilities of requiring any special plant; any special needs for site security or safety; if the contract or job is away from base, how much travelling time or subsistence will be needed; and the position of casual local labour.

Holiday periods Where any holiday periods are involved in the space of a contract, it is usual to allow $6\frac{1}{2}\%$ of the year's working time for holidays, or 2 weeks annual plus 6 days public holidays.

Forecasting, long or short term A long term contract would allow for the introduction of alternative methods of construction or materials, and also for a regular staff to be employed without any drastic fluctuations in overtime. Long term forecasting is essential if materials and operatives are in short supply, or long deliveries are envisaged for materials or components. Short term forecasting would be more common to workshops or the smaller crafts, and would enable priorities to be changed without really affecting the job.

Good forecasting should lower the cost of the job, give higher production with better quality, and reduce wastage.

Programme planning steps (i) Prepare a master plan or programme of all the main jobs which have to be done with some indication of priorities. (ii) Break down each job or phase, with the needs of materials, plant, and labour required. (iii) Consider if any one phase or step requires modification. (iv) After going through the above three steps, prepare detailed plans of men, materials, and plant requirements.

Flow of work For workshops, such as joinery, the flow of work is simple where several items of one size are to be produced. A continuous flow of production would ease any delays and urgent movement of workers, and present regular requirements for transportation. Where any work flow needs a sequence of operations, such operations should follow in a geometrical pattern, (circle or straight lines), so that bottlenecks and distance movement is kept to a minimum.

The flow of work is also dependent on the following characteristics, which will be dealt with in detail later; (i) layout of workshop or site; (ii) the control and siting of materials; and (iii) Time and Motion study factors.

Preparing the plan or programme Generally, any preparatory work will have to consider the full content of work to be done, and the methods which will be employed. On larger jobs, these two requirements will have already been prepared by the team of planners and the foreman can extract from the Bill of Quantities all the items of work related to his trade—collecting the items under the main theme or operation.

Bill Ref. No.	Main Operation	Quantity	Priorities

Fig 1   Preparing the plan

Job break down Start from the main key operation, and break it down or phase it to include all the minor operations or jobs which are associated with that item. Remember that one item may not finish with the production of that single item alone, eg one item of work concerning the joiner may well include french polishing, or the fixing of expensive fittings.

Key Operation	Quantities	Minor Operations	Part Quants.	Time Required	Plant Required

Fig 2   Planning minor operations

Modification After the job has been broken down into items, consider again each minor operation checking the part quantities of materials required for each phase as a fractional part of the overall material requirements.

In estimating the time required, the foreman should think in terms of time needed to perform main operations. For house building, the bricklayer may well have key operations such as: work to damp proof course, work to 1st floor level, work to wall plate level, interior work, partitions. The carpenter might divide his operations broadly as carcase work and finishings, or sub-divide it further as floors, roof, and 1st, 2nd, and 3rd fixings.

It must be remembered that sometimes when work progresses and one would expect production to increase, some jobs then begin to show a reduction in output, eg pointed brickwork above ground level with the forming of openings etc may go much slower than the output which was produced below ground level.

Time Allowance To illustrate the time allowance and aspects which must be considered in planning the programme, a generalised example for an average traditonal house would be as follows:

1. Time on average taken to build   15 weeks
2. Time from start to DPC level   15% } of Total
3. Time from DPC to roofing-in   45% } Working Time

To get a more realistic picture, by making allowances for any unforeseen contingencies and holiday periods involved:

1. Time from start to hand-over: 15 weeks or 75 working days, (on a five-day week).
2. Allow 10% (7½ days or 1½ weeks) for unforeseen events: leaves 13½ weeks or 67½ days.
3. Total working time, (13½ weeks), less allowances for holidays in this period (say ½ week), leaves 13 weeks or 65 days for the actual work to be done.
4. Time to be spent on work from start to DPC level, (15% of total working time), would be 9¾ days.

5. Time to be spent from DPC to roofing-in, (45% of total working time), would be 29¼ days.
6. Time left for finishings, (40% of total working time), would be 26 days.

Note that the time allowed for holidays, may (dependent on time of year), come in the middle of any of the above phases of work.

Detailed plan of men, materials, and plant The foregoing time allowances, accommodate the building or house as a whole, and incorporate all the trades involved. This overall planning would be the responsibility of the general foreman, who would indicate to the craft foreman the position of the overall plan where his particular trade came into it, and from then on it would be the craft foreman's job to plan for his own trade.

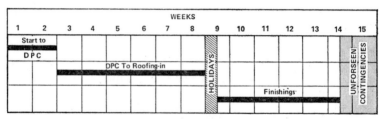

Overall programme for house

Fig 3   An overall programme for a house

The craft foreman's job to estimate the requirements of his own craft force in materials, plant, and men, will be dealt with in detail in the next chapter.

Example: the accompanying two charts illustrate a proposed programme drawn up for the erection of 30 houses in 15 blocks (semi-detached), and to be constructed within 9 months.

Fig 4 shows the site layout and how the stages of completion reached under 5 broad operations, (foundations, carcass roof, finishings, and services), can be recorded either by hatching lines or colours according to a pre-arranged legend key.

Fig 5 shows the dates on which the operation stages were reached for each of the 15 blocks. This record method shows at a glance the general progress achieved to date, and the work which still has to be done.

Short term or weekly site planning Very often in building work, an overall plan or programme has to be changed because of weather, shortage of materials, lack of labour, insufficient plant, or unforeseen contingencies which may arise.

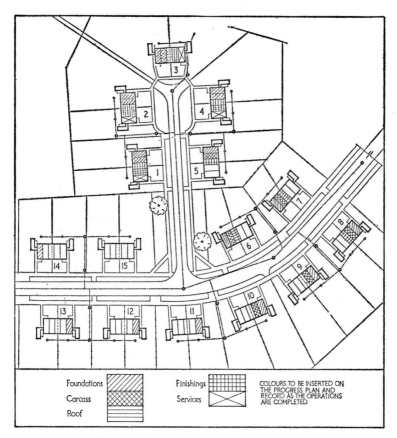

Fig 4   A progress plan for thirty houses

COLOUR REF'NCE	OPERATIONS	BLOCK NUMBERS														
		1	2	3	4	5	6	7	8	9	10	11	12	13	14	15
(hatched)	FOUNDATIONS EXCAVATION, CONCRETE & BRICKWORK TO D.P.C.															
	DATE COMPLETED.	14.4.48	21.4.48	28.4.48	5.5.48	5.5.48	12.5.48	19.5.48	26.5.48	2.6.48	2.6.48	9.6.48	10.6.48	23.6.48	30.6.48	
(crosshatch)	CARCASS BRICKWORK ABOVE D.P.C. 1ST FLOOR JOISTS.															
	DATE COMPLETED	13.5.48	25.5.48	2.6.48	10.6.48	22.6.48	30.6.48	9.7.48	20.7.48	28.7.48	5.8.48					
(vertical)	ROOF CARCASSING AND TILING ETC.															
	DATE COMPLETED.	8.6.48	16.6.48	25.6.48	6.7.48	14.7.48	22.7.48	29.7.48	9.8.48							
(grid)	FINISHINGS INTERNAL PARTITIONS, FITTINGS PLASTERER, PLUMBER, & PAINTER ETC.															
	DATE COMPLETED.	19.7.48	26.7.48	30.7.48	11.8.48											
(bowtie)	SERVICES DRAINAGE, PATHS, FENCES & EXTERNAL CONNECTIONS.															
	DATE COMPLETED	15.7.48	21.7.48	5.8.48	11.8.48											

Fig 5   A progress record for thirty houses (fifteen pairs)

Therefore on large or small jobs, the foreman will be required to keep one eye on the overall programme, and the other on short term planning for the ensuing week's work. Any short term plan must be flexible to cover any of the eventualities listed above, but still follow the original main sequence of operations. A short term or weekly site plan is often the enlargement or detailed plan of that same time portion of the overall plan or Programme.

Making a weekly site plan In making a weekly or short term plan, the following considerations must be made:

Materials Has the current delivery of materials been made? Are the delivered quantities sufficient for the period requirements?

Plant Has the programmed plant requirements been delivered? Are these sufficient for the work in hand? Has the date for existing plant requirements, particularly those on hire, expired, or is an extension required?

Specialist work Has the work of specialists and/or sub-contractors been completed as planned? Will specialists be held up due to craft progress to date? Will extra craft work or further 'waiting' on the specalists be required (which will be a drain on the labour force).

Labour force Is the current craft labour force up to the strength programmed? Is that force sufficient to cope with the work or progress required? With an excessive labour force, is there sufficient work and the necessary materials and plant for their employment?

Preparing the weekly programme The weekly programme is prepared by the foreman one week ahead, and should be compiled after a weekly site meeting with the other craft foremen and sub-contractors under the direction of the general foreman or site manager.

1. List the main operations to be carried out.
2. The number of operatives required for each operation.
3. Indicate any plant requirements, and when needed.
4. Indicate the time requirements for the operations.

Site or Contract ..New Factory........ Craft ....Carpenters................

Week No .....13.......... Week Ending .May 12th Labour Force ...6.....

Job or Operation	Labour Req.	Mon	Tues	Wed	Thur	Fri	Sat
Floor Area No 3 Formwork to Staunchions.	6	▨	▨				
Floor Area No 2 Stripping and moving Formwork.	2			▨			
Floor Area No 4 Erecting Formwork Formwork.	4			▨			
	2				▨		
Floor Area No 3 Stripping and moving Formwork.	6					▨	
Plant Requirements	Crane			X AM		X PM	

Fig 6 A weekly site plan or programme

5. Where plant is extensively required, a daily time-tabled programme can be compiled outlining perhaps hourly requirements.

A simply weekly craft programme example is illustrated in Fig 6 but the method of compiling will depend on the individual foreman and his commitments. With planning completed, the work performance must follow, and its success can only be achieved with good supervision on the part of the foreman.

6

Progress Charts

It will have been seen earlier that when a contractor makes a tender for a contract, he divides his work into a number of different sections or operations, and considers how these can best be carried out, and what each will take or possibly cost in labour, plant, and materials, resulting in a programme.

It will be remembered that a programme is really a forecast of the job or operation, and its essential points should contain: the best method or plan of carrying out the various operations; the order or sequence in which the operations are to be carried out; and the time allocated to each operation.

Progress in building work means the achievement which is realised. The programme is only half the story, being prepared before the work commences; the second half of the story is in seeing that the actual work achievement follows the programme, this would be the progress.

Progressing calls for the following: seeing that plant, labour and materials are on site at the right time; that jobs and operations commence at the time they have been planned; and that there is sufficient plant, (efficiently maintained), and adequate materials on site to supply the labour force.

Programme and progress This is the relationship or comparison between what has been planned, and what has been achieved. This comparison can be made in a visual manner so as to throw into prominence any discrepancy which may arise between the two. This comparison should be made at frequent intervals, so that if any discrepancy arises the issue or fault can be rectified before the programme becomes too disorganised.

The programming must be as accurate as possible and the progressing kept as closely in step and up to date. The form or method of recording the relationship must be such as to be adaptable to enable changes of design and methods to be made in the programme and in the progressing without creating complications in the records.

THE PROGRESS CHART

A progress chart could be defined as a chart prepared by a builder, so that by visual means the progress of the work can be assessed at any time.

Preparing the chart The chart should be as big as possible for clarity. The first stage, is to draft the programme under headings according to the sequence of operations due to be carried out. The operations are listed vertically on the left side of the chart.

To the right of the operations and horizontally, the rest of the chart is devoted to 'time'. The time factor must indicate (on the left) the starting date of the contract, and (on the right) the completion date of the contract.

Against each operation, a line or bar is drawn on the time scale showing the planned time required for that operation. The time bars must be drawn bearing in mind the relationship between operations and trades, and with space allowance for progress to be recorded.

Progress on the programme would be more contrasting and convincing if the time bars were filled in with varying shading using coloured pencils.

Space may also be allocated to show: (i) Actual time taken for varying items of progress made. (ii) The quantity of work done under the progress. (iii) The labour force used in achieving the progress. (iv) Requirements or usage of plant related to progress. (v) The amount of materials used in achieving the progress.

Advantages of programme and progress chart It is a live progressive record of the work done on site. It shows the amount of work involved in each operation, along with the estimated time required for each, with dates of the estimated start and finish of each operation. It shows when the operation actually started, and how much work has been done each week, (assuming the chart is brought up to date each week). It records when steps were taken to boost the production and progress, to try and keep it parallel with the programme. It enables a study to be made ahead of each operation, so that the needed quantity of materials, men, and plant, can be assembled ready for the next operation.

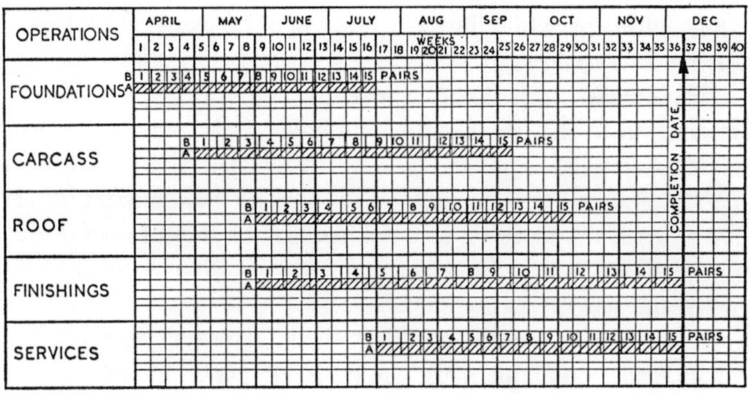

Fig 7   A simple programme chart

Example: The accompanying two charts show simple examples of programme and progress, and are both related to the programme task of erecting 15 pairs of semi-detached houses in 9 months, which was outlined in Chapter 5.

The first chart (Fig 7), shows a recording system outlining the order in which the operations should be carried out and the dates when each stage should be reached. The hatched lines A for each operation, show how long it is estimated the

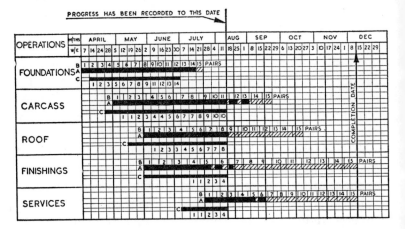

Fig 8   A simple programme and progress chart

work will take, while lines B show when the work on each pair
of houses should start.

The second chart (Fig 8), shows the actual progress achieved
in relation to the programme, and when each stage is reached.
Lines A are filled in or coloured in when the work on each
pair of houses has been completed or partly completed. Lines B
show when the work on each pair of houses should start. Lines
C are the 'Time' lines, and are filled or coloured in to show
when the work was completed.

Reference to the second chart shows that for the operation
of 'Foundations', this work has been completed for 14 pairs of
houses, that the work started a week late, and that the 15th pair
is 4 weeks behind the programme.

The 'roof' operation is in line with the programme, 'carcass'
and 'services' are ahead, and 'finishings' are on the whole a
little behind the programme although work on one house has
started ahead of time.

7

Estimation of Requirements

MATERIALS, TRANSPORT, PLANT, CRAFT LABOUR

It will already have been observed from previous chapters, that from the 'planned operation', or 'work control', or whatever terminology we wish to give job forecasting, that the real aim of any job should be a good foreman with a well balanced labour force, who have been well briefed for their duties. Also well sited materials available on the job when required. A further aim is that where transport and plant are required, the foreman should attempt, for ecomonic reasons, to have full working time for same.

Estimation of materials required Study the Bill of Quantities, and this will give the total quantity of materials required for the job. The bill gives the quantity of materials as taken from the contract drawings, the initial drawings prepared by the architect for the tender price.

For a smaller job, where no bill is provided, study the specification and drawings, and from these produce a list of production quantities required.

As the quantities recorded in the bill are net measurements and take no account of waste, or user waste, or shrinkage, (such as timber, mortar, or concrete etc), the foreman must make allowances for these to the totals recorded in the bill.

The bill of quantities, and the method of preparing quantities from the drawings will be dealt with in detail later.

Before ordering materials from a supplier, the foreman should check on amounts, if any, stored by the firm. It is also important that before ordering any materials, the foreman should check the bills of variation, and the current working drawings, which could differ from the contract drawings.

Ordering of materials Having ascertained the total quantity of materials required, the next consideration is to determine the delivery period and the exact quantity of each item required for these dates. Dates of material requirements, making allowances for delivery from outside suppliers, can be gained from the programme or operation schedule.

Always make allowances to build up stocks in advance of production and especially if the work is going well ahead of schedule, otherwise you will create a waiting period. Whether the materials are to be gained from the firm's stock or a supplier, the foreman should initially check on his firm's method of ordering. Where goods are from a supplier, the official ordering may be done by the office staff, in which case the foreman would be expected to prepare a 'Materials Required Order', a specimen of which would be along the lines shown in Fig 9.

Job or Site ....

Bill Ref.No.	Position	Quants Required	Date Ordered	Date Required	Date Delivered	Comments

Fig 9   A materials required order form

Where the foreman orders materials directly with the supplier, normally 4 copies of the order would be made and distributed as follows:

1st copy (original)—to merchant or supplier.

2nd copy—to head office.

3rd copy—to employer or architect.

4th copy—retention on site or job.

If the materials are extras, or for variations to the contract, the 3rd copy would automatically be sent to the architect.

Transport and plant Normally these items would be requisitioned from a plant department, or hired from a plant contractor. In the latter case, hire rates must be negotiated by a skilled person possibly on the costing side.

The time when the plant is wanted, and the period of retention on site can be determined from the programme. Requisition and delivery to site, should be determined in the same way as for materials. If the progress of work does not proceed at the expected rate, advanced warning for extension of hire or retention should be made to the particular plant department.

Plant—buy or hire If plant is bought outright, there is a good percentage Board of Trade relief. For large contracts, one should buy if the usage is likely to be 55% or more of the contract time. For operational plant, at least 65% of time should be guaranteed before buying.

If the contract is to last more than a year, it would probably be more economical to buy outright and sell afterwards, rather than hire. Choice of petrol or diesel plant is a matter of choice, but generally diesel gives dearer maintenance but fewer breakdowns, and it must be remembered that petrol is always a danger to pilferage.

Example: The accompanying (Fig 10) illustrates the planning of labour and materials as related to the programme task of erecting 15 pairs of semi-detached houses in 9 months, which was outlined in the previous chapter. The chart shows how the programme can be set up for the job as a whole and the approximate labour and materials requirements, extracted from the estimate, set out in the order in which they will be required. This will enable the materials to be ordered well in advance and arrangements to be made for the labour and plant to be on the site at the right times. As the work proceeds, the actual labour strength and deliveries of materials can be recorded, together with the progress achieved in the construction.

MAIN OPERATIONS	SUB OPERATIONS	ESTIMATED LABOUR AND PLANT REQUIREMENTS
FOUNDATIONS	1	EXCAVATION & CONCRETING BRICKWORK TO D.P.C.	7 GEN. LAB'RS 2 BRICKL'RS 1 LAB'R WITH 7/5 MIXER
CARCASS	2	BRICKWORK, TO 1ST FLOOR & 1ST FLOOR JOISTS	8 BRICKL'RS 4 LAB'RS 2 CARPENTERS
	3	BRICKWORK AT FLOOR LEVEL TO CHIMNEY STACKS	5 BRICKLAYERS 3 - LABOURRS
ROOF	4	CARCASSING ROOF MEMBERS & CEILING JOISTS	CARPENTERS 2
	5	TILING & BATTENING	1 TILER 1 - LAB'R
	6	PLUMBING, ELECTRICAL & GAS CARCASSING	4 PLUMBERS 1 ELECTRIC'N
FINISHINGS	7	1ST FIXINGS & PARTITIONS	2 CARPENTERS 2 BRICKLAYERS 1 LABOURER
	8	PLASTERING & 2ND FIXINGS PLUMBING & ELECTRICAL FINISHINGS	7 PLASTERERS 4 CARPENTERS 2 PLUMBERS 1 ELECTRIC'N
	9	PAINTING & GLAZING (SUB-CONTRACT)	5 PAINTERS 1 GLAZIER
SERVICES	10	DRAINAGE, PATHS & FENCES	SAME GANG & PLANT AS FOR FOUNDATIONS

PROGRAMME: WORK TO START SHOWN THUS 1 2 3 ETC BLOCK
PROGRESS (WORK COMPLETED) SHOWN THUS 2 3 ETC BLOCK

ESTIMATED COMPLETION DATE

SUB-CONTRACTOR'S STARTING DATE →

PROGRESS RECORDED TO THIS DATE →

LABOUR	NUMBER OF MEN (EXCLUDING SITE STAFF)		APRIL	MAY	JUNE	JULY	AUGUST	SEPTEMBER	OCTOBER	NOVEMBER	DECEMBER

MATERIALS		TOTAL REQUIREMENTS	DATE ORDERED		APRIL	MAY	JUNE	JULY	AUGUST	SEPTEMBER	OCTOBER	NOVEMBER	DECEMBER
BRICKS	600,000	FEB. 26	DELIVERIES ESTIMATED	100,000	110,000	210,000	150,000	30,000				
			ACTUAL	105,000	120,000	210,000	150,000					
CEMENT	345 TONS	MAR. 24	ESTIMATED	40	60	80	45	40	40	20	20	
			ACTUAL	45	50	85	45					
TILES	120,000	FEB. 10	ESTIMATED		16,000	26,000	26,000	26,000	26,000			
			ACTUAL		18,000	26,000	25,000					

Fig. 10

8

Materials

DISPOSITION AND PROTECTION

If work is to flow smoothly, with the least loss of time and expense in transit or movement, the placing or efficient siting of materials is important. Good disposition of materials means that some planning or forethought has been given to the arrangement of materials, in order to gain efficient performance of work.

Good disposition should help the sequence of operations or flow of work; permit the work to be done speedily because of efficient handling; and ensure orderly work, and the prevention of site or shop congestion. The good siting of materials is also dependent on a good site or works layout.

Site Layout The suggested pointers below may also have some bearing on workshop layout, where appropriate.

Consider site clearance before planning layout, so that any trees under preservation order, will not be disturbed.

Entrances or exits should give good access to vehicles or likely plant.

All entrances, exits, and site roads, must be sited to avoid congestion or bottlenecks.

Provide for the extension of the site, or build-up of stocks or delivery of materials.

Site layouts should prevent the least disturbance by movement of traffic, noise, dust, or smell, to the public or adjacent properties.

Beware of the transfer of clay or soil to adjoining roads in bad weather.

Allow sufficient room for internal transport and production in progress as well as adequate room for operatives.

Consider the requirements and existing provisions of water, electricity, and telephone etc.

Materials Layout

Avoid double handling or unnecessary movement.

Site the materials not to interrupt the production of work.

Stores for components should be as close as possible to site workshops and offices for ease of administration.

Consider any security necessary against possible theft by workmen or public.

Consider the possible damage or deterioration to materials by exposure to weather, and damage to fragile components.

Site or store materials to prevent waste, (see later notes).

Consider the layout in relation to the use of services, ie water, current, light etc.

Consider the layout of any plant which may be needed in conjunction with the use of some materials, ie power saws, or mixers etc.

Make the best use of natural lighting for mixing bays or site workshops.

Provide adequate storage for materials which easily rust.

Arrival of materials on site The foreman himself or a responsible person to whom the delegated responsibility has been given, should ensure that all goods and materials delivered to site conform to the quality, quantity, and type required or ordered. The following actions, some of which will be dealt with in detail later in Chapter 22, should be carried out: delivery notes should be checked for accuracy before being signed; unload the materials and stack or store according to the planned layout; delivery notes should be retained or forwarded to head office according to the system practised by the firm; and check the quantity of materials received against the quantity required on the Materials Required Schedule, (see later notes).

Causes of material waste Poor workmanship; defective materials due to lack of checking on receipt; damage through poor or unsuitable storage; excessive supplies, or delivery before being wanted; rough handling, bad transportation, or bad dumping; lack of salvage or recovery on any site movement; and failure to collect any rejects or breakages for return. Check on the return of suspected empty crates or containers which still may contain components.

To prevent careless handling of materials encourage respect for them, and avoid movement. Provide where necessary suitable lifting and transporting gear. Ensure that operatives and labourers are informed of storage and stacking arrangements. For small components, introduce suitable containers or improvise from empty drums or crates.

Defective materials Establish a thorough method of inspection on receipt. Ensure that the material complies with requirements or specification. Return any rejected materials on receipt, and adjust the delivery note accordingly. Where the defect is found on use, check on the terms of sale and the method of return or getting replacement.

Bulky or finishing materials Ask for delivery only when required or when suitable protection can be provided. Watch the progress of work, so that perhaps a roof or partially completed part of the building can afford protection on delivery. Do not destroy any packing material, ie straw, paper, or cardboard etc. It may be useful later for the protection of completed work or other materials.

Protection of fixed materials It is impossible to generalise because of the varying types of fixed materials in different trades, but the following isolated examples may give some leads:

Adequate use of priming paint on site fixed joinery.

Laths or sacking on rebates or arrises.

Tape, lagging, or gummed paper, on furniture, fittings, or sanitary goods.

A standby of sacks of sawdust or chippings to cover floors in bad weather.

A roll of roofing felt or plastic sheeting is always a good standby for quick protection or bad weather protection.

In jobbing work, the use of old or removed materials for protection of new work (old doors, boarding etc).

Considerations in plant siting Provide a level base for mixers etc and wedge wheels to prevent movement. Mixers etc should be sited adjacent to material bays. Some locations may be dependent on position of water and electric supply.

Always afford adequate space round plant or machines for cleaning and maintenance, and provide adequate space for plant fuels which are needed. Give consideration to the protection and safety of fuels, and site so as not to endanger parts of the building or adjacent inflammable materials. Site petrol and diesel plant so that the smell and fumes are not dangerous. Beware of staining materials or parts of buildings with exhausts or leakage of fuels, (danger of oil staining). Consider security of plant and fuels (starting handles, belts, plugs, and taps, might be kept in a site office or under the foreman's care).

The question of scaffolding will be dealt with separately, (see Chapter 15).

9

Plant and Machinery

OPERATION AND MAINTENANCE

Any tool, plant, or machinery, kept in good condition makes work easier and is an asset to production. It is essential that any form of equipment or plant should always have fair treatment, and never be roughly handled. Cleanliness of plant or machine is essential, and if defects are found they should be dealt with immediately. Regular inspection of all equipment in use or on site must be carried out. It is also essential that inspection is made before equipment is sent out from a yard or workshop to site, and similarly on return. Proper maintenance not only means the oiling of moving parts, but that defects should be reported or repaired as soon as detected.

The foreman's responsibility concerning plant He is responsible to his employer to ensure the best possible full use of equipment. Before commencing work on any site, acquaint yourself with the site's safety officer and his instructions, or site requirements. The foreman must ensure that all plant and equipment is maintained in good working order, earning money and not costing money; ensure that the best use is made of hired equipment during the hiring period; and ensure that all equipment is serviceable and safe for all operatives, and in no way dangerous to the public.

Make sure that adequate and the correct type of equipment is provided for each operation or job. Allocate responsibility for the maintenance of plant or equipment to competent operatives, and ensure that they are well informed to report any faults or defects to the foreman.

Competent plant and machine operatives Any type of mechanical plant, or machine, does not itself cause accidents. It is usually the operator who is incompetent. The definition of a 'competent person', as quoted by the Royal Society for the Prevention of Accidents in the 'Construction Regulations Handbook', 7th Edition, is as follows:

> The person chosen should have such practical and theoretical knowledge and actual experience of the type of machinery or plant which he has to examine as will enable him to detect defects or weaknesses which it is the purpose of the examination to discover and to assess their importance in relation to the strength and functions of the machinery or plant.

Inspection and maintenance of tools and equipment It would be impossible to deal in detail with the tools and equipment which are peculiar to the varying trades, so to generalise, the following items which are common to most trades are outlined:

Cold Chisels—kept sharp, but avoid the formation of dangerous mushroom heads.

Spades—the blades should be kept clean, rivets tight, and split or damaged handles avoided.

Hammers and picks—inspect for missing, loose, or improvised wedges.

Hose-pipes—should be kept off the ground, 'bridged' to prevent wear in heavy traffic positions.

Pneumatic Tyres—the correct air-pressure should be maintained.

Mixers, Buckets, Spray-guns etc—should be well cleaned after each day's use.

Barrows—should be washed daily, and tyres and wheels well maintained.

Trestles, Ladders, Saw-horses etc—kept under cover when not in use.

GENERAL PLANT

Heavy plant and equipment, or that needed by specialists, is beyond the scope and context of this publication, and maintenance of the more general items are given below.

Scaffold boards should be cleaned at least every month, and hoop-iron binding or wire examined for possible renewal; should not be used for situations which might damage or distort the board, such as skids etc; and split or rotted boards should be discarded. Ensure that all personnel know that boards should not be dropped or thrown from lorries or scaffolds. Never saw up long boards to make short ones, there may be weaknesses which are exposed.

Ladders Regular examination should be made for dangerous or worn rungs, or missing wedges. Regular painting could be dangerous in covering up any defects—a varnish or similar should be considered as a preservative. Carefully examine extension ladders for rusted fitments, or worn or rotted cords.

Ropes Avoid knots in rope, dry after site use, and store in a dry place, and never coil when wet.

Wire ropes and chains Examine chains for worn links, and ropes for broken wires. Try to prevent knots in chains, and kinks in ropes. Store in dry place, and keep well greased to prevent rusting.

Metal scaffolding Fittings should always be stored under cover, and regularly examined for distortion or worn threads. Aluminium tubes need no maintenance, but should never be heated. Avoid the use of damaged tubes, these could be cut to make shorter ones or putlogs. Do not attempt to straighten bent or distorted tubes without the use of a special machine. Steel tubes easily rust, periodical brushing or cleaning is essential and painting considered.

Trestles and steps In use, step ladders should never be used to support the weight of more than one man. Use a trestle instead. Examine the treads or rungs, and cords and hinges for wear and rusting respectively.

PLANT MAINTENANCE

Whatever the type of plant, the maintenance programme should follow a three-stage routine: (i) A daily or weekly check by the user or operator, which should include cleaning, oiling, greasing; topping up fuel, oil, and water; and the tightening up of loose nuts and bolts. (ii) A regular inspection by a qualified mechanic to ensure running efficiency. (iii) A periodical service or overhaul, when the machine or plant should be stripped down and completely overhauled.

The foreman and plant maintenance Make one operative responsible for all the craft plant, or the individual responsible for the plant under his use or control. Ensure that adequate instructions are given for daily or weekly maintenance to be carried out, and ensure that each operative is informed and is conversant with the use and maintenance of the plant or machine in his charge. Any relevant manufacturer's instruction book or maintenance manual should be issued to each operator.

Always allow adequate time and space on site for cleaning, maintenance, and repair. If plant is to be laid up for any length of time, especially after winter months on site, or prior to winter use on site, ensure that all exposed parts are coated with a suitable rust preservative.

Plant and machine records Keep a record card for each machine or item of plant, if possible with a recording of dates and hours worked, and any form of maintenance or repairs carried out, again with dates.

The above information would provide a valuable check on running and maintenance costs, and also indicate when the next servicing was necessary. Record a report every week on the general use and condition of each machine or plant, or of orders connected with repairs, spare parts, or servicing.

Check on any plant manufacturer's servicing scheme, and keep records of such servicing carried out. Check on any insurance which the firm may have to cover plant or machinery, and that the necessary insurance company's inspections are carried out.

Machine or Plant Item					
Date	Parts Serviced	Parts Replaced	Special Oil or Lubricant	Next Service Due	Serviced By

Fig 11   A plant or machine record

Test certificates It is required by law that Test Certificates for lifting and hoisting equipment and pressure vehicles, should be maintained in a general register. (See later notes under 'Safety Regulations'.)

E

10

Incentive Schemes

PRODUCTIVITY AND CRAFTSMANSHIP

Incentives have been defined as, 'an appeal to human nature which arouses feelings and incites action'. There are two fundamental types of incentive: (i) financial, which provide an encouragement through giving extra remuneration for better production, effort, or results. This payment, could be applied for individual piece-work or to a group on a profit-sharing basis; (ii) non-financial, an incentive which offers no financial reward, but gives prospects of promotion, or better working conditions etc.

The aims of any incentive scheme At the outset, there shall be an accurate measurement of the work which is carried out. The administration of any scheme must be uniform, irrespective of the work involved. Any scheme should include all employees and not be limited to those carrying out repetitive work. All schemes should provide for a guaranteed minimum weekly wage in order to offer a means of security, and the financial appeal should be sufficient to incite more effort or production.

Any scheme should have some controlling factors governing standards and quality, as well as maintenance time for machines or plant, otherwise any of these may suffer. Any method used in caluculating the incentive in terms of financial gain should be simple to understand by the workers. All incentive rates should be agreed and put in writing before any work starts. Any forms of rate-cutting should not be allowed, once an agreement has been reached, otherwise this may create a precedent and snowball.

Rates should not create excessive earnings which cannot be maintained, or cause friction because they cannot be earned. Provision should be made in any incentive scheme to allow for a revision of the rate should there be any change or alteration in the nature of the work. Opportunity should be made to allow the worker to participate in discussions as to how the rates are determined, or to express genuine grievances.

The foreman and incentives Although a foreman may disagree with any form of bonus or incentive, particularly if he is on a standard wage, or if he considers that any such scheme may lower the quality or standard of work, he must show interest and see that such a scheme works if it is the policy of the firm.

Even with an incentive scheme, the foreman's job is still to get the work completed with maximum quality and output at the least cost; to try and get a right proportion or fair play to work done for the employer as well as pay to the operative; and although basic wages are regulated by local or national agreement, the foreman may still have to administer the wage structure impartially so that rewards are related for skill according to the nature of the work being done.

The foreman's duties in incentive schemes Ensure that the workers know their targets, and understand the agreements fully. Ensure that quality and standards are clearly defined, and that it is understood that shoddy or inferior work would be a breach of the agreement, with possible loss of bonus. Ensure that any queries on measurements or other factors involving bonus are settled as quickly as possible. A bonus scheme can only succeed effectively if the working conditions are right, with proper disposition of materals and plant.

Results of good incentive schemes should lead to more thoughtful planning, which if carried out well, could result in a better organised job. More thought given to size of craft force, and materials required on the job and their delivery, in order to keep the scheme or output going.

Because the operative will know what is expected, both individually and collectively as a craft force, he will unconsciously gain a picture of the job's plan and progress.

A well organised incentive scheme, with full support of all the working force, (who are satisfied because they are gaining financial rewards), should result in a successful job.

Advantages of group incentive It encourages team-spirit among the operatives; enables costing systems to be simplified; enables men to be moved from one job to another; and prevents the need to have several individual piece-rates, which because of their difference may cause friction.

Disadvantages of group bonus payment It could lead to a complex computation of wages. The individual is not likely to give of his best under any group-sharing scheme, and it could result in friction between workers because they think they are doing more work than others in the group. Difficulties may arise between operatives as to how such a scheme works, or on measurement.

VARYING INCENTIVE SCHEMES

Every type of incentive scheme or plan, seeks to do one of several things, increase productivity, raise standards of quality, reduce waste, and in some cases help to distribute profits.

Types and characteristics
Payment on performance of a job or operation, which would demand accurate assessment.
Payment on individual performance, good for the individual but not for teamwork.

Group performance, which promotes team spirit but not individual effort.

Immediate cash rewards, provides an attractive but only a temporary bonus.

An interval bonus, given perhaps at quarterly, half or yearly intervals, is not very rewarding except on a long term basis.

Small basic wage with high bonus, would not be very encouraging to slow workers or new operatives.

High basic wage with low bonus, would tend to produce a regular work performance and be attractive to the operative of below average ability.

Setting the Rate Decide first if the type of work demands an incentive because production requires speed more than other factors. Consider if the job can be considered as a standard or uniform project, and the possible working time for performance.

Attempt to average operatives working speed if for a group bonus, or the working speed of one operative if the incentive is for individual performance. One method of assessing an individual working speed is to equate one hour to a constant of 100, and if the working speed of one worker was considered to be 75% that of a normal worker, then the working speed on a job of that operative would be his time actually taken by 60 (minutes), and multiplied by 75.

In attempting to assess any forms of timing, one should consider the element of fatigue, lifting, exterior weather conditions etc, also that in a normal working day the time lost for short breaks and use of toilets has been considered to vary from 3—10%.

After considering all the above factors, the incentive rate should be set. In doing so, it must be remembered that if hourly rates change, incentive rates must change too.

Incentive rates and agreements
As building workers are associated with many employing

authorities, it must also be remembered that there are some trade union agreements which set down that any incentives are not less than a given percentage minimum above existing time rates.

Payment methods

There are many different types of payment or premium plans, some of which came into being as early as the end of the 1800s, and may have characteristics suitable for varying types of industry. The 'Rowan' Plan of 1898, has been considered to be fairly generous to workers, as it worked on the system of 'times saved on time allowed was multiplied by the time wages'. Some bonus systems allow a proportion or fractional part of the time saved on a job to be paid at the ordinary rate to the worker. Example: Under the 'Halsey' System, one-third of saving time is allowed to the worker, so if the operative's rate was 60p per hour and he completed a job in 6 hours for which 8 hours was allowed:

Bonus equals 1/3rd (8 − 6) x 60p giving 20p or £0.20.

11

Training Apprentices

STARTING NEW EMPLOYEES

Apart from starting apprentices and introducing them to the building trade and their training, the foreman may be responsible for engaging new employees and assigning them to duties, and on engagement should try to create a friendly impression, so make the new operative feel at ease, and remember that first impressions can be lasting ones. Put yourself in the new worker's place, and treat him as you would wish to be treated. Gain some personal information concerning his background, or experience or training, which may be useful later in your approach to him or in assigning work. Enquire about his education, if an apprentice, whether he has attended a pre-apprenticeship or similar course, his hobbies, and any possible connection with the building trade.

Outline rules and regulation Give details of starting and finishing times, break and meal periods. Show him the location of toilets, canteens, stores, place for tools and clothing, and first aid provision. Outline any site dangers or special regulations. If an apprentice, explain to him the deed requirements and details of the probationary period, and the length and conditions of his apprenticeship.

Outline the firm's policy Show each new operative round the site or workship. Outline the type of work required of him, from whom he takes instructions, and where he can obtain tools, materials, or plant etc. Outline the quality and standard of work required.

If an apprentice, explain the organisation of the firm, the co-ordination of trades, and the firm's method of promotion; methods of dealing with any problems or difficulties; and any details concerning protective clothing, meals or canteen facilities, and transport to site.

Methods of work and payment Outline instructions on production; wage rates and method, time and day of payment. Give any information of special rates such as overtime, or bonus or incentive schemes. Inform the operative of time sheet entries or other forms of records needed, and the means of submitting same.

Explain the percentage of wage rates as they apply to trainees, labourers, or apprentices, and inform apprentices about technical college attendance, or other forms of training. Ensure that everything under this heading is fully understood, to prevent any initial misunderstandings.

Acquaint new operatives with craft force Introduce the new worker to his immediate superior such as charge-hand or shop-steward and introduce him to other craft workers, specialists, or sub-contractors, with whom he will come in direct contact.

Information required of new employees (i) His last firm and details or reasons for leaving, if you feel this is important or may have any bearing on redundancy pay. (ii) If sent from the Ministry of Labour, has he the necessary card and insurance cards? (iii) If changing jobs, what influenced the change, further experience, individual contact by an employee, or by reading an advertisement published by the firm? (iv) Check on references, or an apprentice's school reports. (v) Check on employment card if the apprentice has been sent from the Youth Employment Officer. (vi) Check on any contributions to holiday or pension schemes, or Income Tax Code number or locality of last Tax Office—which will be useful information to pass on to the firm's office.

APPRENTICES

If the firm has any vacancies for apprentices, they should first notify their local Youth Employment Office.

Apprentice quota The following quotation is taken from the London Master Builders' Association publication, 'Guide to Craft Apprenticeship':
To provide for the steady flow of skilled craftsmen essentially needed for the Building Industry of the future, it is desirable that where possible every employer should employ 1 apprentice to every 5 craftsmen in any one trade, providing the proportion in the whole trade employed in the area shall not exceed 1 to 7. If adequate training facilities are available and all the apprentices are properly indentured, application may be made to the Joint Committee to exceed this quota.

The apprentice and training An extract from the National Form of Agreement, para 3 states: 'The Master and the Representative are satisfied that the Apprentice is a suitable person to be taught and instructed as an apprentice in the craft of ....'. This is indeed a challenge to the employer in his selection of the apprentice.

Probationary period Apprentices should serve a period of probation not exceeding six months. During this period, the foreman should watch the apprentice and get reports of his progress from the other operatives and from the technical college, in view of the Deed requirement that he 'is a suitable person to be taught'. If the apprentice appears to be unsuitable for his craft, the foreman should be truthful with the employer and the parent or guardian, and terminate the probationary period.

Training the Apprentice The Deed states that the employer or master shall, 'during the said term and to the best of his knowledge, power, and ability, to teach and instruct the Apprentice or cause him to be taught and instructed in the Craft of ....'.

The foreman as a manager, should be concerned that any form of training is done properly. In selecting operatives to train the apprentice, the foreman should consider those who have the following qualities and ability: (i) are competent craftsmen and can inspire confidence and skill; (ii) are methodical in their work, tidy, and capable of controlling the apprentice; (iii) can instruct and impart the skills of the craft with safety, yet point out the dangers; and (iv) the operative must have a desire to instruct the apprentice, and be able to judge his ability or aptitude and progress.

Planning the training Check on the type of local technical college courses—if day or block release, the latter will call for some adjustment in the site or workshop training. Decide on what skill or capabilities you expect the apprentice to have acquired by a certain time (so that you can assess his progress). Try to provide a variety of experience, and attach the apprentice to different operatives. The variety of experience should, where possible, include site, jobbing (or shop work), and at varying periods of the apprenticeship. Always show an interest in the apprentice's work, his college work, and examinations.

The apprentice and wages

The scale of wages, which are proportions of the appropriate standard craftsman's rate, are laid down in the Deed of Apprenticeship (see Chapter 29). No apprentice under the age of 18 must work overtime, over the age of 18 they may work overtime if it does not interefere with attendance at evening classes.

The apprentice wages should be paid in respect of his attendance at a technical college course. Wages shall be paid to the apprentice for an aggregate period of four weeks in any one year for absence through illness or injury contracted at any time, providing a doctor's certificate is supplied. This part of the Deed must be stressed to the apprentice as each year many lose wages for long periods due to prolonged absence from work as a result of injuries received from participating in sport.

Apprentice training and bonus schemes Wherever possible the apprentice should not be employed on jobs where individual bonus or incentive schemes are operative, because of restraint on training. Where a team bonus is operative, the apprentice too should benefit at his percentage rate. Where there are short periods of time spent on bonus work (due to other training), or where there are difficulties in assessing the apprentice's proportion of bonus, some quarterly or yearly remuneration might be offered.

Where a bonus scheme is regular, and likely to be for a long period, which would present restricted training, the apprentice should be transferred to another job or site. Where the bonus scheme is limited to operations, or the work is repetitive involving little or no training, the apprentice could be directed to individual project work. Where the foreman is not personally involved in bonus work, he could perhaps control the apprentice training himself.

12

Work Study

Work Study is the name given to the method or techniques used in making an analysis or measurement of work done in relation to time. This study is done not only to reduce the effort used in operations, but also to provide vital information for the future planning of work, a basis for incentive schemes, and for producing estimates.

Work Study has also been defined as follows: it is a systematic method of improving working conditions by observing people at work, and recording and measuring what they do and how they do it; it is a commonsense application of management and organisation; and it is the study of an operation or process, to ensure the best possible use of the worker and material resources available.

All foremen (competent or otherwise), have at some time or other practised work study probably unconsciously in carrying out the following: altering sequences of operations or conditions of work; moving operatives from one job to another because of pressure of work or required productivity; deciding how long a job will take, or how many operatives are needed to carry out a job; and by experience, deciding on alternative methods of work.

The above actions gained by experience or tradition, are valuable except in situations where unusual types of work are involved. Where work is of a repetitive nature, eg industrialised or system building, and is not dependent on forms of experience or tradition, this is where initially work study would be of great value.

Work study is comprised of two main parts, which are closely connected, method study, and work measurement.

Method study This is to determine the method or movement content in an operation of how aspects of work are done. There are several ways or devices in which men or material movement on a job or site can be measured, some of which are:

1. Scale models of the site: A model of the completed site is useful in determining suitable positions for disposition of plant and materials, and the movement of same in any one phase or operation. Site movement of vehicles, disposition of soil or excavated material, and the capacity reach of cranes etc could be determined from such models.

2. Flow diagrams: A graphical method which could be done on scaled graph paper to outline the flow or sequence of operations, which would clearly show the lack of movement leading to bottlenecks or excess movement leading to delays.

3. String diagrams: Useful on scale models of site or workshop layouts to show extent of movement of men and materials.

4. Film records: This is likely to be done by a specialist team, who would show by movie film the variance of movement in operations by adopting different methods.

5. Mocks or prototypes: These are useful operations where one hopes to improve on an operation's time rather than cost.

Other methods of method study include those which would be carried out by specialist teams, gaining information from statistics of similar or previous jobs, and Activity Charts or Activity Patterns produced after a job has been done.

Work measurement This is a study analysis to determine the actual work content of any job or operation, and can be gained from the following:

1. Detailed Observations, in which the entire job or operation is timed in relation to what is done and how it is done.
2. Random Observations, which may cover methods of construction, a section of repetition work, or to discover time wastage.
3. Statistics of Previous Work, which would be useful to prove time increases in terms of bad working conditions, or possible decline of work operation time due to labour shortage or inexperienced operatives.

WORK STUDY AND THE FOREMAN

Although work study may be frowned upon by some operatives as a means of spying on them, a successful study analysis can be a useful tool to help the foreman in his duties of getting things done efficiently. A study which showed good work results would reflect favourably the good abilities of the foreman to his employer.

The foreman and work study teams The foreman's co-operation with any work study team could help them tremendously with their task, especially with information concerning changes in materials or methods, or even operatives; reasons for low productivity, if such is justified; and any practical information on operative skills, or the performance of materials.

Benefits of work study to the foreman It would provide vital information which could help to assess work methods and time factors for the preparation of work programmes. Where work study has been carried out, in setting any targets the foreman would know that any performance estimates had been professionally assessed on work already done. After work study has been done, any set targets should be accepted as being fair (or be more acceptable than if no study had been carried out). From the above factors, there should be more generalised satisfaction both to the foreman and workers.

Application of work study to site work Foremen can become victims of the theory that craft work requires no need of work study because of past years of experience or traditional methods. Some operatives will oppose work study because inefficient methods pay them better where bonus schemes are used. Where work study is introduced, it must be 'sold' to the men, and explained that because of it better wages could result through bonus, because more productivity has been achieved.

Where work study is required Work study would be particularly needed where the quality of work was irregular because of the use of unskilled or semi-skilled labour, also where work demands the increase of new materials or new methods of work, or where there has been no past experience of similar work or data to work on.

Carrying out method study Method study can be carried out by the foreman on any job at any time along the following lines: (i) decide on an operation which you want to analyse in comparison to its traditional form; (ii) examine carefully the traditional method being used, and the time required to perform the operation; (iii) plan the job along new lines, new time factors, and new methods of construction; (iv) outline the new plan to the operatives, and put it into operation carefully assessing the result; and (v) if the new method has been successful, stick to it and avoid returning to the old method.

Work study and incentives Although incentives may attempt to prevent work study being carried out successfully, incentives have still to be accepted. It was in 1947, that an agreement was made between employers and operatives that bonus schemes be introduced in the building industry.

Work study decides work content, and ultimately leads to the setting of the piece rate.

Method study decides the magnitude of the operational force and the work which has to be carried out, which would ultimately fix the target hours.

Example on work study

Operation: To unload 4,000 bricks from a lorry on site, and stack them a distance of 3m away.

Present method: One man is used to pick up 4 bricks at a time off the lorry with the help of the driver, and to walk with them to stack 3m away.

Object of study: To consider if time and effort used in walking can be saved by using a roller or conveyor as follows:

Proposed method: One man to erect a roller conveyor between the lorry and stack, and later stack the bricks after removal from the conveyor on which they have been loaded by the lorry driver.

Time studies of the two methods are outlined below:

Present Method:

Operation	Distance in Metres	Time in Minutes
Pick up 4 bricks		0.03
Carry bricks to stack from lorry	3	0.04
Stack the bricks		0.04
Walk from stack to lorry	3	0.04
Total for one complete operation	6	0.15
Repeat the operation 1,000 times	6,000	150

Proposed Method:

Operation	Distance in Metres	Time in Minutes
Assemble roller conveyor		1.50
Stack 4 bricks from conveyor		(0.60)
Repeat the operation 1,000 times		60.00
Dismantle the roller conveyor		0.60
Total	Nil	62.1

Conclusions:

	Present Method	Proposed Method	Saving
Total Time (minutes)	150	62.1	87.9
Total Walking (metres)	6,000	Nil	6,000

F

13

Co-operation between Crafts

Co-operation is essential if full team spirit is to be maintained and the full operative force is to be marshalled into an effective working force. This co-operation must also exist if the policy of the firm is to be successfully put into operation, if there is to be a better working atmosphere, and if there is to be a close relationship with specialists and sub-contractors.

What good co-operation will achieve Apart from the more generalised characteristics outlined above, good co-operation within crafts, and between crafts, should lead to a full co-ordination of the working force, which should result in the following:

Better team spirit promoting output and efficiency.

Less wastage of time by waiting for liaison.

Better discipline, responsibility, and response to authority.

A promotion of goodwill and better understanding in disputes.

The intelligent use of labour which will promote efficiency, yet flexible enough to overcome any difficulties.

Better 'waiting' on other trades, or help given, because goodwill exists.

Information and instructions between trades will be more easily passed on.

A prevention of waste of materials because of omissions, or

failure to provide for installations by other trades (because of the good liaison).

A better economic use of communal plant, tools, or equipment.

Enable short-cycle operations, where combination of trades are involved, to be co-ordinated into combined operations.

Good co-ordination of trades should lead to maximum production and thus lower the costs, with the possibility of better bonus rates.

Any form of co-operation between trades should allow improvements of methods and ideas in tackling jobs.

Co-operation between craft and general foreman Good co-operation at this level is the real start of employment management, and should enable confidence, information, instructions, and responsibilty to be exercised and designated. It should determine conditions and hours of work, and enable internal rules, conduct, and actions based on the firm's policy to be fixed. It should determine policy to be made on piece-rates, bonuses, and agreements, and enable the strength of the labour force to be planned, along with training and recruitment, and enable liaison between crafts, specialists, and sub-contractors, for the improvement of work and production. Co-operation should provide a channel for the interchange of ideas and suggestions.

Outline the site requirements for safety, health, and welfare, or any other special provisions required, and prevent misunderstandings, or a circulation of incorrect information. This should enable not only employment management, but better management to ensue, remembering that 'all democratic processes are to some extent an insurance against bad management'.

Co-operation and better site management This enables targets, standards, and quality of work to be set. The sequence of work can be planned, and loss of time and wastage of materials prevented. Priority of work can be formulated, and workers placed in operations best suited to their ability. Combined detail planning can be made, which will enable better forecasts to be made for manpower and material requirements, and enable discussions to be made on expected stage completions of trade work. This means the prevention of site difficulties, delays, and grievances, and enables the arrangements to be made for casual labour to assist with materials, scaffolding, or plant movements. It enables dates to be fixed for the requirements of staging for specialists and sub-contractors.

Co-operation would enable reactions to be expressed and discussed fully, resulting in common decisions which would be in the interest of all. It would enable any lack of information or weakness in planning to be known, discussed, and overcome.

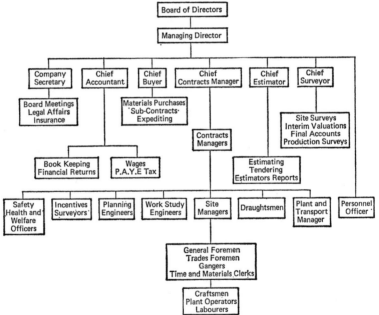

Fig 12   The organisation of a building firm

THE ORGANISATION OF A BUILDING FIRM

The organisation and constituent members of a building

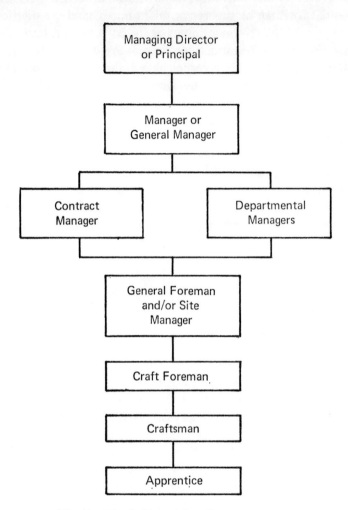

Fig 13   The ladder of building management

firm varies according to the size, policy of firm, and the type of work carried out. The two accompanying charts illustrate varying organisation, with that at Fig 12 showing management, workers, and administrative staff, while Fig 13 shows the ladder from apprentice to managing director.

The construction and supervisory team In order that the potential foreman or supervisor might understand the division of responsibility, the main duties of the construction team and those responsible for supervisory work are outlined below.

General Manager He is responsible to the managing director or principal of the firm for the overall organisation and control of work. He would be the firm's liaison officer with client, architect, or planners, and would sign the contract on behalf of his firm.

Contract Manager He controls and co-ordinates the work of the production team which includes management staff, operatives, specialists, and the supply of plant and materials.

Planning Engineer He is responsible for the breakdown of any building project into a system of operations or programme of work, together with the calculation of time factors involved and methods of construction to be employed.

Departmental Managers According to the size of the firm or magnitude of a job, it may be appropriate to appoint departmental managers for each of the various crafts as well as plant, transport, maintenance and personnel, and they would be responsible for the working of their departments to the general manager.

According to the size and organisation of each firm departmental managers may include the following: works manager, small works manager, joinery manager, painting manager, plastering manager and plumbing manager.

Site Engineer On large sites, a site engineer, who by profession is usually a structural or civil engineer, would be responsible for the overall setting out and accuracy of the site, and the testing and strength of materials. He would be responsible to the contract manager.

Quantity Surveyor He is responsible to the contract manager for the presentation of information concerning costs. His duties are to measure and value work completed against targets; the assessment of work variations; the value of work done by specialists or sub-contractors; and the operation of any bonus or incentive schemes.

Estimator This member of the team produces estimates of costs involving an assessment of the technical, operational, and contractual aspects of a building project.

Buyer or purchaser This member of the team deals with the schedules of materials required for a contract, by obtaining quotations for same, negotiation of price, placing orders, and obtaining deliveries.

Site Agent The site agent is responsible for all the site personnel which include all administrative staff as well as the production staff. Sometimes the term 'Agent' is applied loosely or wrongly to other supervisors.

General Foreman or Site Manager According to the size of the site, there may be more than one general foreman or site manager, who would be responsible for all site work and the control of all the trades, specialists, and sub-contractors. Usually a site manager would be resident on site and in charge of all operations.

External Parties involved with site organisation

Clerk of Works He may be appointed by the employer or architect to act as an inspector on their behalf. His duties are to see that the materials and workmanship connected with a contract agree with the contract's drawings, specifications, and design. In the course of his inspection, he could test, or arrange for testing, any material that he may consider necessary, and also check on any form of setting out.

Resident Engineer A resident engineer is usually a civil engineer by profession and employed instead of a clerk of works on a contract where the work is of a civil engineering type rather than normal building work. On a large contract where both types of work may be carried out, a resident engineer as well as a clerk of works may be employed to supervise their respective interests.

Building Inspector A builder must notify the local authority of the proposed commencement of certain types of work, and must not cover up such items as drains and damp-proof courses until inspection has been made. It is the function of the building inspector, who is employed by the local authority, to see that such items described previously, and any form of structural work is carried out in accordance with the building regulations and any other local by-laws which may apply.

Public Health Inspector Where building work is related to alterations, repairs, or maintenance, the craft foreman may come in contact with the Public Health Inspector, who is employed by the local authority. His main duties are to enforce the requirements of the Public Health Acts, and the Clean Air Act.

Factory Inspector The Factory Inspector associated with building work would be employed by the Ministry of Labour, and his duties are to ensure that the statutory requirements of the Factories Acts, affecting sites and workshops, and covering such items as safety, health, and welfare, are carried out.

14

Continuity of Work

BAD WEATHER PERIODS

Building in this country can be very hampered in winter time by uncertain weather, and it is during this period that about 30,000 to 50,000 workers in the construction industry are normally laid off work. Bad weather is given as the reason for rising unemployment and falling production in the winter months, and this has been a feature of the industry for so many years that there is a tendency to accept the disruption caused by bad weather as a natural part of the building scene, and this is accepted by too many employers. Over the years, the amount of production lost through bad weather is much greater than that lost by strikes.

Winter Building The Government has given a great deal of publicity to this problem, and the Ministry of the Environment along with the Building Research Station have published much information on aspects of winter working methods. Winter building has been made prominent on television, and the Meteorological Office has provided weather forecasts to local builders so that they can take precautions against changes in local weather conditons. The Economic Development Committees for the Industry have also discussed ways whereby the Industry can be persuaded to adopt appropriate winter working methods on a much wider scale than at present.

Wintry Conditions

Rain during prolonged periods may entail the transfer of men from outdoor to inside work.

Frost may occur any time between late October and early March, and could cause a stoppage of concreting or bricklaying.

High Winds may hinder the use of cranes, or damage fresh brickwork or partly constructed roofs.

Fog may cause a delay of men and materials, and is probably worst around the industrial areas in November, December and January.

Snow, usually the danger months would be December and January, and with frost could bring sites to their worst conditions.

Preparation for bad weather Have a supply and issue protective clothing, and have portable heaters for drying out, especially the interiors of buildings during frost. Build up stocks of sand or gravel to deal with icy conditons for transport on site, or entrances or exits. Hold a supply of tarpaulins, roofing felt, or plastic sheeting for the protection of materials, and a supply of sawdust or shavings for floor protection is always a good asset in muddy conditions.

Precautions during frosty periods Extend curing time or accelerate the hardening of concrete. Drain water from cooling systems of engines to prevent damage. Use anti-freeze. Remember that it is possible for radiators to freeze while engines are running and it is wishful thinking to drain and refill daily. The labour cost involved in refilling will more than cover the cost of anti-freeze. In severe frost, where concrete work is being done, heating the water and aggregate and mixing in close proximity to the job should be considered. New brickwork, blockwork, formwork moulds and reinforcement bars should be covered and protected. Consider wind-breaks for mixing bays, and try to get work done quickly, particularly those jobs associated with the trowel trades.

Planning for continuity of work It is difficult to generalise what should be done in order to plan in advance for continuity of work under wintry conditons, especially as any form of preparation would vary according to the different trades, some of which are more affected than others and the following pointers may help as a guide:

Try to time the peak periods when fog, frost, and snow, are likely to affect building work.

Prior to the possibility of frost periods, concentrate on the completion of large scale brickwork and concrete work.

Concentrate on completion of roofs, and roofs being covered in before peak times.

Try to leave any fixings or interior work as long as possible during the late autumn (especially trowel trades).

Ensure the glazing or the covering of door and window openings before frost periods.

Whatever the trade (and this is not easy, except perhaps for the larger firms), try and plan a reserve of repairs, jobbing, or alteration work involving interiors. These jobs are not easy to hang on to until bad weather comes, remembering also that clients may not want such jobs done during inclement conditions.

For the trowel trades in particular, the foreman should keep a check on weather forecasts and temperature levels.

The following temperature levels may prove useful guides:

Reading	Guide
0°C	Water freezes, and hardening of concrete and mortar stops.
4°C	Minimum temperature for placed concrete or mortar.
10°C	Rate of hardening is reduced below this temperature level.
13° to 25°	The best range for concrete or mortar.
30°C	Too high a temperature for concrete or mortar, which may result in flash setting.

Where site work is impossible Under extreme wintry conditions, it may be possible for short periods to employ men on the following (where applicable): (i) painting or maintenance of ladders, trestles, and plant; (ii) the inspection and maintainance of scaffolding and components; (iii) full maintenance and servicing of plant; and (iv) possible transfer to shopwork for carpenters and plumbers.

Site Lighting Winter brings its loss of daylight to the normal working day, and this alone accounts for the loss of one-tenth production every year between November and February. It has been estimated that artificial lighting is only used on ten per cent of civil engineering sites, and about one-third of general building sites. Poor lighting not only causes a loss of production, but contributes also to the accident rate. A survey on accidents in the construction industry published by the Ministry of Labour shows that some accidents might well have been prevented if additional lighting had been used.

Site lighting can be provided by various forms of equipment, which operate on paraffin or similar fuel, liquid petroleum gas, generated electricity, or mains electricity.

The foreman can gain plenty of information from suppliers of the above first three forms of equipment, should it be his responsibility to provide artificial lighting. If a mains supply is required, the foreman should give as much notice as possible to the local Electricity Board. A charge will be made for a temporary supply, but where a cable exists the supply would no doubt be provided by the Board after a contract with the Board has been made.

Electricity Requirements Information on Lighting in Buildings can be obtained from Code of Practice No 321. A private generating plant should conform to BS Code of Practice 323. Where a transformer is used, with an output voltage higher than 25 volts, it should conform to BS 171 and where this does not exceed 25 volts, the transformer should conform to BS 3535.

Site Heat Heating for sites and jobs may be needed for other than welfare requirements [to be dealt with later], and especially for winter building in the following situations: the drying out of buildings or newly used materials; the bulk warming of materials; and the defrosting of ground, equipment, plant, or formwork and shuttering.

Apart from winter use, site heat is sometimes required to deal with dry rot spores in walls etc. The foreman can gain much information on equipment of varying types which would deal efficiently with any of the above situations, from the many firms who supply liquid petroleum gas.

Weather Forecasts The foreman can do much to help himself in the planning for continuity of work in winter or bad weather, by gaining a warning in advance from weather forecasts. The foreman should acquaint himself with his nearest local meteorological office, from which weather forecasts may be obtained by telephone and in some cases at any time of the day or night. Met offices and weather information centres, are also prepared [sometimes with charges] to provide short period or monthly forecasts or climatology services. This would help with the planning stages of any operations.

Summer Bad Weather Period Although the winter months are frowned upon by the building industry as being the most difficult for continuity of work, and the side effects of unemployment and loss of production, it must also be remembered that hot, dry, summer weather could also be classified as a bad weather period.

A hot, dry, summer period would present the following difficulties and problems for the foreman:
1. Premature drying times for concrete work, which would require damping-down or cover.
2. Dust caused by site transport can upset the painters as well as the public or adjacent owners, perhaps the re-routing of vehicles might be considered.
3. Hot weather will also prolong the drying of certain materials such as: (i) glazing putty, which may extend the

time before painters can operate; (i) the blistering of new paintwork; and (iii) bitumastic materials such as felts, DPC's, and surface treatments, which may hold up further work.

The above situations could perhaps be prevented with the provision of sun-screens.

4. Heat will encourage shrinkage of joinery items, and also provide the ideal situation for '2nd Seasoning', which if encouraged would reduce the former.

5. Working in hot and dusty conditions, will create tiring situations for the operatives especially if the worker is in a static position, so movement and shade must be considered by the foreman.

6. Good weather encourages the lack of protection of materials, the foreman must remember that any good spell of weather can suddenly break resulting in materials being ruined.

15

Scaffolding

ERECTION AND MAINTENANCE

Scaffolding on a large scale or big job would normally be carried out by a specialist firm with the foreman becoming less involved, even so the foreman will have to deal with the provision of scaffolds on small jobs and sites, and the safety requirements involved.

Types of scaffold Although there are several forms or adaptations of scaffolds, there are two main types:

Putlog consists of a single row of standards, which are set approx 1.300m from the outside wall of a building, which partly helps to support the scaffold (Fig 14).

Independent consists of a double row of standards, which are set about 1.050m apart, and which do not depend on on the building or wall for support (Fig 15).

Other forms or adaptions

Cantilever or Trussed Scaffold are generally one lift scaffolds, although in some instances several lifts may be erected.

Suspended Scaffold.

Chimney Scaffold.

Roofing Scaffold for roofing work generally.

Birdcage Scaffold interior scaffolds for work below ceiling heights.

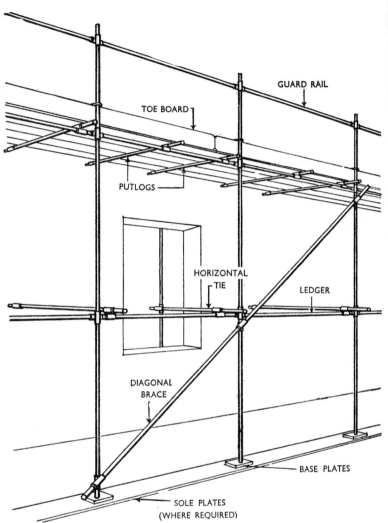

GUARD RAIL

TOE BOARD

PUTLOGS

HORIZONTAL
TIE

LEDGER

DIAGONAL
BRACE

BASE PLATES

SOLE PLATES
(WHERE REQUIRED)

Fig 14 A typical Putlog scaffold

Slung Scaffold hung from the underside of roofs, where it
is impracticable to scaffold from ground level.

Mobile Scaffold where the height should not be more than
3 times the width of base.

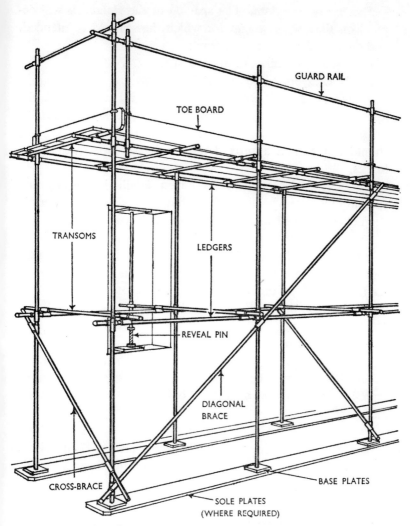

Fig 15 A typical Independent tied scaffold

Prefabricated Scaffold where the units are fabricated into usually 'H' shaped interlocking frames.

Scaffold members and components are shown with their application in Figs 14 and 15.

G

Spacing of Standards The spacing of the standards will depend on the use or weight for which the scaffold is intended, and the following are suggestions:

For masons—1.200 to 1.800m apart.

For bricklayers—1.800 to 2.400m apart.

Standards 2.400m apart the load should not exceed the approx weight of 2 men, 50kg of mortar, and 80 bricks.

Standards 1.800m apart the load can be increased, but should not exceed approx 2 men, 50kg of mortar, and 140 bricks.

Safety Note Not more than 2 men should be on any one span at any time when loaded as above, and no other materials should be wheeled or carried across such loaded spans.

Intermediate Putlogs For Putlog scaffolds, intermediate putlogs will be required according to the thickness and length of scaffold board (in order to support them), as follows:

Thickness of board	Max spacing of putlogs
30mm	925mm
38mm	1.500m
50mm	2.650m

The boards must be supported at a distance of not more than 4 times their thickness from their ends in order to prevent the boards tipping.

Bracing or stiffening of scaffolds must always be provided where pulley-blocks or lifting appliances are fitted to a scaffold, or when placing heavy loads upon a scaffold.

Dismantling Scaffolds
1. Tubes or fittings should never be dropped to the ground, all scaffolding should be lowered carefully and stacked flat.
2. Collect fittings in sacks or bags.
3. When not in use, tubes should be cleaned and stacked.
4. After fittings have been checked, they should be soaked in light oil and, if possible, stored in drums.

MINIMUM WIDTHS OF WORKING PLATFORMS

Types of scaffold	*Min width*
On outside of sloping roof	425mm
Platforms suspended from, or supported by a roof	425mm
Suspended scaffolds raised by winches	625mm
Other suspended scaffolds as defined	425mm
Ladder and trestle scaffolds for light work	425mm
Temporary platforms passing between two adjacent glazing bars of a sloping roof and used for work only in vicinity of such bars	425mm
(ditto if the above space does not permit)	625mm

Other scaffolds	
When used only for a footing	625mm
When used for materials as well as for footing	850mm
When used for support of another platform	1.050m
When used for dressing of stone	1.275m
When used to support another platform and for dressing or rough shaping stone	1.475m

Working Platforms must extend 600mm beyond the end of a wall.

Scaffold boards should be not less than 200mm wide; extend not more than 4 times the board thickness beyond the support; be fitted with bevelled pieces (to make rigid) where necessary; and rest on 3 supports or putlogs.

Guard rails must be provided if the platform is 1.950m or more in height; must be 900mm above the platform; and must be not more than 675mm above the toe board.

Toe boards must accompany the guard rail, and must be 200mm high or more.

Ladders must extend 1.050m above the platform and must be on a firm footing. They must be secured or tied to prevent slipping. Defective ladders must not be used.

Timber scaffold boards The specification requirements for Timber Scaffold Boards made from sawn softwood, 38mm thick by 228mm wide, are contained in British Standard 2482:1963. The specification outlines species of timber, growth rings, slope of grain, permissible knots, wane, distortion and damage.

Estimated scaffold requirements An Independent Scaffold in relation to a Putlog type would require

Twice as many Standards
Twice as many Base Plates } as the Putlog type.
Twice as many Ledgers

16

Safety and Welfare

Everyone connected with the building industry, whether they are employers or employees are well aware of the position that the industry holds in the table of industrial accidents.

ACCIDENTS

For years, there has been an annual average of over 40,000 reportable accidents and over 200 killed, with higher percentages than in all other industries. Building workers suffer over 3 accidents for every 100,000 hours worked. If this rate is to continue, every worker in the industry can expect to be injured twice during his working life.

Accidents in the industry cost the country millions of pounds a year in: (i) the need of scores of hospital beds per day; (ii) a drain on medical staff and services; (iii) a drain on union and insurance company funds, and (iv) a loss of thousands of man days to production.

The above statistics are from accident books and reports, and although statistics can be explained away with words of higher production, the situation is still serious.

In order that the foreman may play his part in accident prevention, a guide to accident causes and prevention are listed overleaf:

The Causes of Accidents (General to all trades)

1. Ladder accidents.
2. Falls of materials.
3. Falls from roofs.
4. Falls from working platforms.
5. Collapse of excavations.
6. Transport accidents.
7. Machinery accidents.
8. Protruding nails.

Accidents can be prevented by improving the working environment, the guarding of machines, better site organisation, the setting up of safety committees, and better interior lighting.

Responsibilities to safety by the employer Although the foreman has his own responsibilities to safety, he must also know those which apply to the employer, and where possible encourage and help him to carry them out.

The employer must see that his men, and those employed on his site, are protected from unnecessary accidents. He must realise that accident prevention is a top managerial problem, and the responsibility must not be pushed to supervisors. He must appoint at least one Safety Officer, where 20 men or more are employed. Although to provide plant and equipment in the interest of safety costs money, the failure to comply can cost compensation, valuable time, and heavy fines. The employer must beware of the use of 'green labour' on sites where there are likely to be greater dangers or hazards. This would apply where industrialised methods are used rather than traditional.

Accidents must be reported. In one year recently, the Ministry of Labour disclosed that only 60% of accidents that should have been notified, had in fact been reported.

Responsibilities to safety by the employee Building workers, due to the nature of their jobs, are tough men—they have to be—and yet this may be one reason why they are not always aware of dangers involved in their work. Each year the industry loses, through accidents, too many men in their thirties and forties, who are badly needed because of their skill and experience.

The foreman could do much to bring operatives to realise

their responsibilities to safety by encouraging (i) wearing the correct protective clothing for the job in hand; (ii) reporting any unsafe situation or deficiency to him or the safety officer; (iii) where anything is amiss (such as a protruding nail), correcting it; (iv) the correct use of tools and plant for the job; (v) following manufacturer's instructions on all tools and machines; (vi) obeying all safety signs and safety instructions; and (vii) older tradesmen must repress skylarking and inculate safety consciousness among younger workers.

Responsibility to safety by the safety officer Firms with 20 men or more engaged in building operations, or works of engineering construction, are required by law to appoint at least one safety officer or supervisor who is responsible for safety supervision. He should be conversant with the legislation and list of documents given in this section, and his main duties are:

Periodical inspection of work to check that statutory requirements for safety are observed; promotion of safe working conditions; investigation and recording of accidents; promotion of safety training within the firm or site; and production of an annual report to the firm's management, and to advise on future safety.

The foreman as a safety officer The National Federation of Building Trade Operatives have stated that a foreman should not undertake any appointment as a safety officer. His job as a foreman is a full time one and he cannot give priority to safety duties as required by the regulations. Possible conflict between production duties and safety duties would rule the foreman out of taking on such a position. The NFBTO suggest that if an employer persists in trying to appoint a foreman as a safety officer, the facts should be reported to a factory inspector, who would back the foreman on this issue.

In the execution of his duties (with or without a firm's safety officer), the craft foreman will have to ensure that certain safety measures in the way of operations, plant, equipment etc are carried out.

The main approach to any form of legislation by the foreman is to know that a regulation exists for all building operations, and the second best thing to knowledge is knowing where to find it. It should be stressed to the foreman that all relevant documents relating to building regulations or legislation of any kind should be amassed by him as part of a personal library, and these should be kept on site for immediate reference. It is to this end, that a list of official documents is appended later in this chapter.

In the interest of safety, the foreman should acquaint himself with site safety signs and posters and use these in every situation which presents itself. The first set of Safety Signs produced by the NFBTE in 1970, are illustrated in Appendix 2.

At all times, the foreman might try and impress on others what has been described as the 'Big 5' attributes to site accidents:

1. Manual handling of goods.
2. Falls.
3. Stepping on, or striking against objects.
4. Incorrect use of hand tools.
5. Skylarking, or the human element of the lack of concentration.

Apart from the human failure, which is everyone's concern, the two main causes of accidents in building work are faulty methods of work, and untidiness of sites. Both these situations are covered by regulations, and the foreman can do much to see they are implemented.

REGULATIONS, NOTICES AND REGISTERS

The Building (Safety, Health and Welfare Regulations), 1948, SI 1145.

(a) Para 1–4, General Information and Interpretation.
(b) Para 99, Registers, Certificates etc.

The Construction (General Provisions) Regulations, 1961 —1580.
  (a)   Plant and Equipment and Materials.
  (b)   Demolition and Explosives.
  (c)   Excavations, Timbering, and General Safety.
  (d)   Lighting of Working Places.
  (e)   Fencing and Machinery.
       To be held in site office.

The Construction (Lifting Operations) Regulations, 1961 —1581.
  (a)   All Lifting Appliances Design and Construction.
  (b)   Erection and re-erection.
  (c)   Chains, Ropes and Lifting Gear, also Annealing.
  (d)   Signalling and Selection of Personnel.
  (e)   Carriage of Persons.
  (f)   Hoistways, Towers and Fencing thereof.
       To be held in site office.

The Construction (Health & Welfare) Regulations, 1966— 95.
  (a)   Canteens.
  (b)   Drying Rooms.
  (c)   Toilets.
  (d)   Protective Clothing.
  (e)   Washing Facilities.
  (f)   First Aid.
  (g)   Form 2202.
       To be held in site office.

The Construction (Working Places) Regulations, 1966— 94.
  (a)   Scaffolds.
  (b)   Ladders.
  (c)   Duties of Sub-Contractors.
       To be held in site office.

OFFICIAL FORMS AND PUBLICATIONS
(Supplied by HM Stationery Office)

The following forms and publications to be held at builder's office:

Form 11, Permissible Hours of Work for Women and Young Persons.

Form 36, General Register for Building Operations.

Forms 55, 55a, 56, 57, Test and Examination of Steam Boilers, Economisers and Superheaters.

Form 58, Examination of Steam Receivers.

Forms 59 and 60, Examination of Air Receivers.

Form 75, Certificate of Testing and Examination of Hoist.

Form 80, Certificate of Tests and Examinations of Crabs, Winches, Pulley Blocks, and Gin Wheels.

Form 91, Part I, Records of weekly inspections, examinations, and tests of Scaffolding, Excavations, and Lifting Appliances.

Form 91, Part II, Records of reports on thorough examinations of Lifting Appliances.

Form 92, Register of persons employed in painting buildings, (Lead Paint Act, 1926).

Form 96, Certificate of Test and thorough examination of Crane.

Form 97, Certificate of Test and examination of Chains and Lifting Gear.

Book BI 510, Accident Book, (National Insurance Act).

The following forms and publications to be held on site:

Form 43, Notice of Accident (S 80), or Dangerous Occurrence (S 81) to be sent to Inspector.

Form 41, Notice of Poisoning or Disease (S 82).

Form 91, Part I, Sect A, Inspection of Scaffolding.

Form 91, Part I, Sect B, Examinations of Excavations, Shafts, Earthworks etc.

Form 91, Part I, Sects C and G, Inspection and Examination of Lifting Appliances.

Form 91, Part I, Sect D, Test for security of Crane Ballasting.

Form 91, Part I, Sects C and E, Inspection of Automatic safe load indicator.

Form SI, 1145, The Building (Safety, Health, & Welfare Regulations, 1948).

Posters, Placards and Leaflets for site or workshop:

Form No F901, Placard—Warning Notice of Fragile Roof covering.

Form No F954, Electricity Regulations.

Form No 988, Woodworking Machinery Special Regulations.

Form No 996, Lead Paint Regulations, 1927.

Leaflet No 1008, Advice on First Aid Treatment.

Leaflet No F2080, Building Operations (First Aid Boxes) 1959.

Leaflet No 2041, First Aid (Standard of Training).

Leaflet No F394, Prevention of Lead Poisoning in Painters.

(A full list of Government publications and forms can be obtained from HMSO).

17

Setting out Buildings

MEASURING EQUIPMENT

Setting out or checking the setting out of work, is the responsibility of the foreman, and its normal craft nature will vary according to the craft concerned and the type of work involved. The setting out of buildings could well be the responsibility of any foreman especially if he is an acting general foreman, or in a similar supervisory capacity.

Building Line The setting out of any building, must meet the approval of the local authority in relation to the authority's 'Building Line'. The local authority will always give information on the exact position of the building line, if a proposed building can be 'set back' from this line, and if they would regard bay-windows etc to project (as is usual) or be considered an 'encroachment' on the line.

Improvement Line The illustration of the block plan of an actual bungalow (at the proposed stage), shown in Fig 16, shows three interesting features: (i) only the extreme corner of the front of the L-shaped bungalow touches the building line due to the direction; (ii) the building line changes direction slightly twice on this example; and (iii) the building line runs parallel to an 'Improvement Line' which in this example, would provide for road widening at a later date. As the improvement line is within the property boundary, the client

108

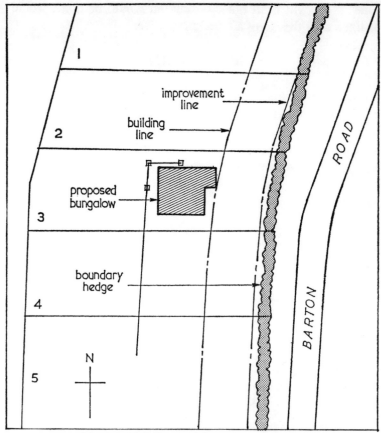

Fig 16   Building and improvement lines

would 'surrender' some of his land to the local authority.

Although the building line is of vital importance in the initial setting out of the building, the improvement line may have a bearing on the position of services, stop-cocks, and hydrants etc in order to accommodate them when the road widening is eventually carried out.

Axial Line When a building has to be set out with special position in relation to the compass, it is likely that the complexity would demand the assistance in the setting out from the architect, and that the main setting out line or 'Axial

Line', from which all other setting out would be done, would be fixed with the aid of a theodolite.

SETTING OUT

Once the building line has been established, this line will be the face or frontage line of the building, and with this frontage line fixed, the remainder of the setting out is dependent purely on parallel lines and right angles. Right angles can be set out by use of one of the following methods or instruments: (i) The Builder's Square; (ii) The '3:4:5' method; (iii) The Optical Square; and (iv) The Site Square.

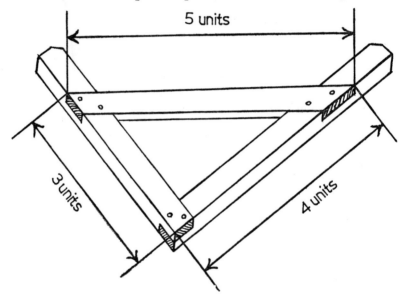

Fig 17   The builder's square

The Builder's Square This should be made of selected, treated, or painted wood with screwed joints, and the 90 degree angle periodically tested for accuracy. The illustration in Fig 17 shows the square, and its application is shown in Fig 19, to the setting out of the 90 degree adjacent line to the building line.

The '3:4:5' Method This method employs the mathematical
Theorum of Pythagoras, (the square on the hypotenuse being

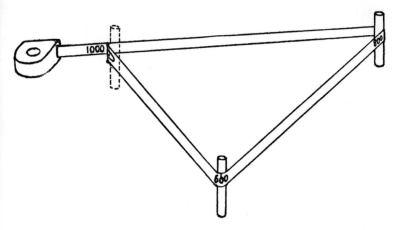

Fig 18   Using a tape for the 3:4:5 method

equal to the sum of the squares of the other two sides), or in
simpler terms, the sides of a right angled triangle being in the
proportions of 3:4:5. This method using a metric tape is
shown in Fig 18, and its application is illustrated in Fig 19.
As shown, two pegs or rods are inserted on the building line
at A and B, which are any multiple of 3 units apart. Then
(with the same units of measure) arcs of 4 and 5 units are
struck out respectively from A and B, which gives an inter-
section at C. The line A—C is at right angles or 90° to
the building line, and a dimension along this line will give
the required depth of the building, (at H and similarly at
E).

The Optical Square is an accurate setting out instrument,
which is illustrated in elevation and section in Figs 20 and 21.
About the size of a pocket compass, the optical square consists of a two-slit line of sight at A and B with a 90 degree
reflected line of sight at C. The mirror X is fully silvered, but

that at Y is horizontally half-silvered and half-clear. To use
the instrument in relation to the setting out shown in Fig 19,

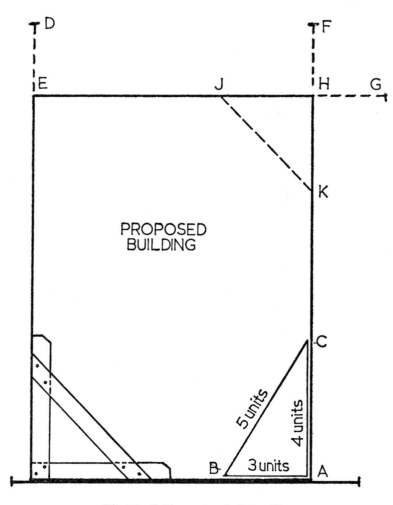

Fig 19   Setting out a building line

the square is set up on a short ranging rod at H with a rod
at J seen in the line of sight.

An assistant with a ranging rod at K then moves the rod
to the left or right as necessary until the reflected image of

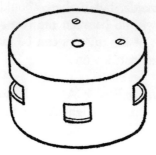

Fig 20   The elevation of the optical square

rod K is seen to coincide with the rod at J—thus the line H—K is at 90° to the line J—H.

To test the accuracy of the Square (refer to Fig 19 again), and from H the rod at J is viewed, and the rod at K is lined in. The position is then reversed, from H view the rod at G and again line in rod K. If the square is accurate, both points

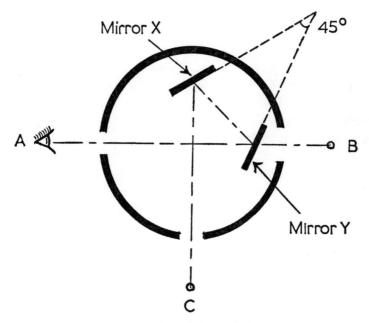

Fig 21   A section of the optical square

H

of rod K will coincide, but if there should be a discrepancy the true position will lie between the two results, and adjustment to the angles of the mirrors can be made by turning the screws on top of the instrument.

The Right-Angle Indicator Although not mentioned as a setting out instrument, the Right Angle Indicator, which is a

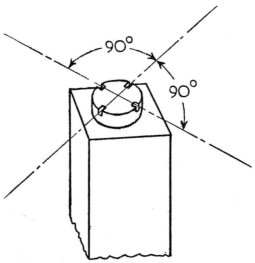

Fig 22   The right-angle indicator

component part of the Quick-Sight Level, can be used for setting out right angles. Fig 22.

To use the Indicator (i) Place the 'Quick-Sight Level' nose down on any level surface. (ii) With the eye approximately 600mm from the instrument, line up two opposite 'notches' in the eyepiece with any known line such as a building line, face of a building, or rods. (iii) Leaving the instrument in position, walk round the Indicator and read off the right angle to the left or right as desired, and which could be fixed by sighting a ranging rod in the opposite diagonal 'notches'.

The Sight Square The Sight Square is illustrated in Fig 23, and is a very simple and reliable instrument which is claimed

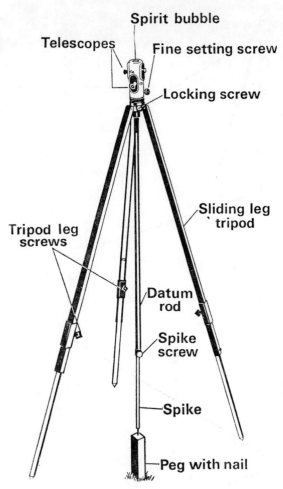

Spirit bubble

Telescopes

Fine setting screw

Locking screw

Sliding leg tripod

Tripod leg screws

Datum rod

Spike screw

Spike

Peg with nail

Fig 23   The site square

to set out right angles to an accuracy of 1 in 4,800. The square is basically two telescopes set at right angles to each other, mounted on a tripod, and plus a fourth leg or 'datum rod'. The 'datum rod' terminates in a spike, which is pointed at one end for use on marks while the opposite end is hollow for use on the nail of a peg. The setting up and use of the site square is well illustrated in Fig 24.

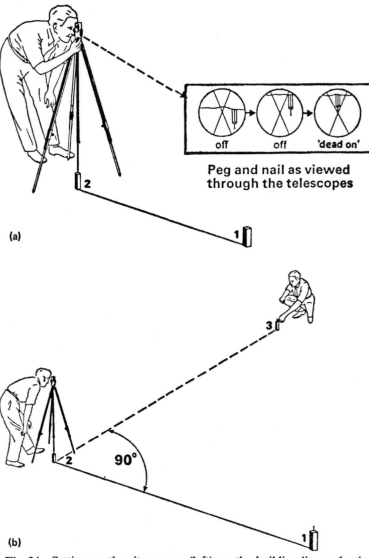

Peg and nail as viewed through the telescopes

(a)

(b)

Fig 24   Setting up the site square (left) on the building line and using the telescope to peg one and (right) after turning the square 90° the telescope is used to fix peg three

Checking After all rectangles have been set out, the diagonals should always be checked (Fig 25), ensuring that

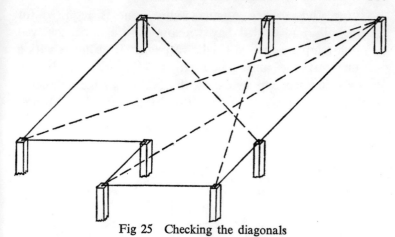

Fig 25 Checking the diagonals

the tape or means of measuring is kept truly horizontal Where a linen tape is used, this should be checked at intervals with a steel tape to ensure accuracy of the dimensions as the linen tape with use will tend to stretch. In setting out large buildings where dfficulty may be experienced in long diagonal checks, the building might be divided up into several smaller rectangles for convenience.

Sloping Sites Difficulties will always be encountered in setting out or taking horizontal measurements on sloping ground, and in order to prevent inaccuracies being made,

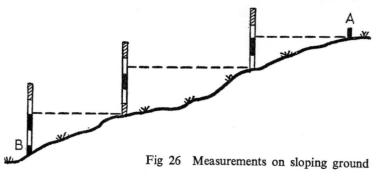

Fig 26 Measurements on sloping ground

Fig 26 shows a suggested method of taking shorter stepped dimensions between ranging rods.

Setting Out Angles Angular setting out is required for squint walls and angled bay windows and can be achieved by using templates, made by the carpenter, from main setting out lines. If the angle required is 45°, this can be set out by using the hypotenuse of the builder's square [assuming this bracing piece has been set at this angle], while 30° and

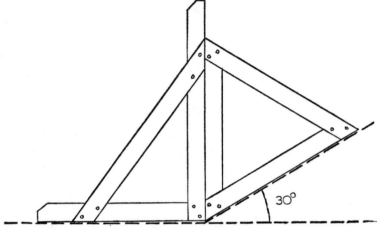

Fig 27   Setting out a 30° angle

60° angles can be set out using an equilateral triangle made of wood in combination with the Square as shown in Fig 27.

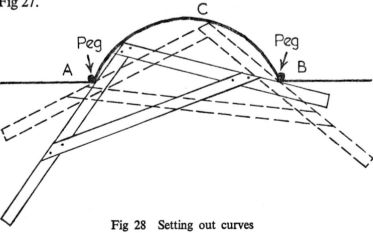

Fig 28   Setting out curves

Setting Out Curves Circular, segmental, and elliptical curves are required for bay windows, paths, kerbs, roads, retaining and boundary walls. For small size examples, prepared wooden templates may be used similar to the application of a wooden triangle in Fig 28, which shows the setting out of a segmental curve with A—B as the span and C as the rise, and with round pegs to ease the movement of the template in tracing the curve.

To find Curve Radius for large curves which are circular or part of a circle, a tape, chain, or trammel, can be used as

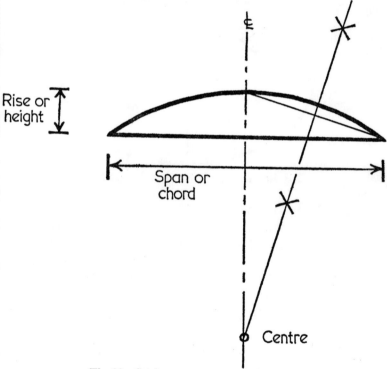

Fig 29   Setting out a segmental curve

a radius arm. If the span, or length of chord, and rise or height of the curve is given as in Fig 29, the radius can be found as follows:

$$\text{Radius} = \frac{(\frac{1}{2}\text{ Chord})^2 + (\text{Rise})^2}{2 \times \text{Rise}}$$

Setting Out the Ellipse Although there are several methods which can be used for the geometrical setting out of the Ellipse, which can be found in most geometrical text books, there are two practical applications which lend themselves to site setting out:

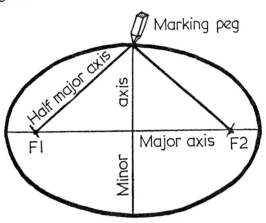

Fig 30   The ellipse by the string method

1.   The String Method:
   - (i)   As shown in Fig 30, the major and minor axes (long and short diameters), are set out at right angles to each other and bisecting each other.
   - (ii)   Half the length of the major axis is struck from one end of the minor axis to cut the former at points F1 and F2, which are known as the Focal Points.
   - (iii)   Nails or pegs are inserted at the Focal Points.
   - (iv)   String (or rope, surveyor's chain, or tape) is attached to one peg F1, and after passing round a marking peg held at one end of the minor axis, is then attached to the second Focal Point F2, and the tension held.

(v)   The marking peg is then moved to described one half of the Ellipse.

(vi)   The loose loop is then transferred to the opposite half of the Ellipse and the operation repeated to complete the shape.

2.   The Trammel Method:

(i)   The major and minor axes are set out as described before.

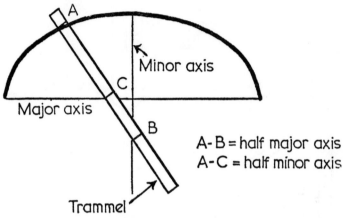

A-B = half major axis
A-C = half minor axis

Fig 31   The ellipse by the trammel method

(ii)   A piece of wood or Trammel is then marked with a dimension equal to half the major axis A—B, as shown in Fig 31.

(iii) From one end of the above dimension, mark off half the minor axis A—C.

(iv)   The Trammel is placed on the axes as shown, with one mark C on the major axis and the other B on the minor axis.

(v)   The Trammel is moved, always keeping the above two marks on the axes, and the third mark A will trace out the shape of half the Ellipse.

(vi)   The operation is repeated in the other half to complete the Ellipse.

Profiles After the initial setting out of the angles of the building has been completed, the next stage in setting out is to form and erect Profile Boards, which will give the width of the foundation trench and the thickness of the walls.

The illustration shown in Fig 32 shows the setting up of a profile for an external angle with saw-cuts provided for lines which would provide the trench and wall widths. The

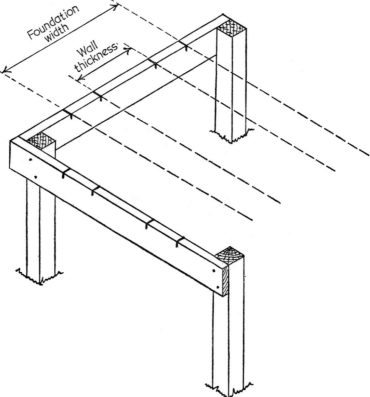

Fig 32   The setting up of profile boards

profile boards must be fixed sufficiently away from the actual external angle to provide for working space.

On level ground the fixing of profiles present no problem, but where uneven ground is encountered a levelling instrument, to be described later in the Chapter on Levelling, may be used or a line and line-level as shown in Fig 33.

18

Levelling

USE OF SURVEYOR'S LEVEL

In various jobs related to building work, the elevation or difference of height of points above the earth's surface is required, and the name given to this operation of determining these differences is known as 'Levelling'.

Levels are needed for the following building operations:

Taking horizontal levels on sloping sites by using a line and line-level as shown in Fig 33.

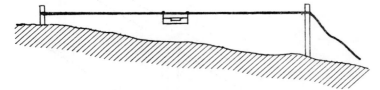

Fig 33   The use of a line level

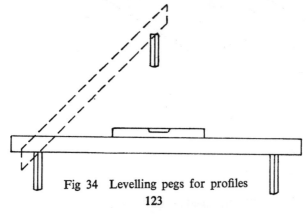

Fig 34   Levelling pegs for profiles

Site levelling for setting out pegs or profile boards as shown in Fig 34, where a straight-edge and spirit-level are used. The relative fixing of levels for brickwork courses, steps, or floors, by using a water level, which is illustrated in Fig 35. This method is accurate because the fluid contained in two glass or transparent tubes connected with

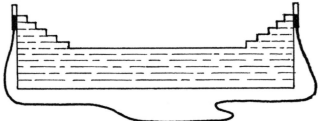

Fig 35   Fixing levels of brickwork courses with a water level

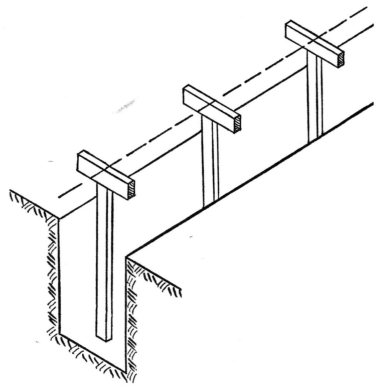

Fig 36   Boning rods used for trenches

a length of tubing and completely filled with water will always find its own level. This method is useful for finding two level points where a wall or undergrowth divides them.

Excavations, trenches, the invert level of drains, and kerbs etc can be levelled below a 'Sight Line' by the use of Boning Rods as shown in Fig 36. Boning Rods which are coloured for ease of sighting and also provided with plumb bobs for ease of being held vertically have been shown in Fig 37.

Surveyor's Instruments More complex methods of establishing a sight or level line on a building site (to which the ground levels of points on the site can be related), are fixed

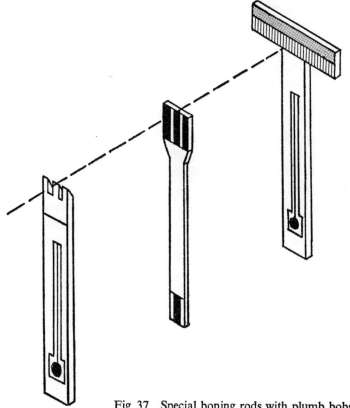

Fig 37 Special boning rods with plumb bobs

by using more elaborate instruments which include: the Dumpy Level, the Quickset Level, the Cowley Level and the Quick Sight Level.

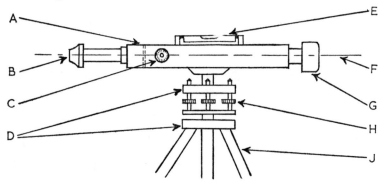

Fig 38 The Dumpy Level: A—position of diaphragm, B—eye-piece, C—focusing screw, D—parallel plates, E—spirit level, F—line of collimation, G—object glass, H—foot screws, J—tripod

The Dumpy Level as will be seen in Fig 38, the Dumpy Level [so called because of the smaller and more compact types compared with earlier versions], is basically a telescope which is mounted on a tripod, with certain other attachments to facilitate its adjustment for use. The telescope is focused by means of a screw which moves the Object Glass. Near the Eye-piece is the Diaphragm. This is a metal ring to which is attached the 'Cross Hairs' or thrust wires—the horizontal one indicates the line of sight or the 'Line of Collimation'. The telescope is capable of rotation on a spindle which is attached to the upper part of two parallel plates, the two plates being kept apart by 3 or 4ft screws. When in use, the lower parallel plate is screwed to the tripod head.

Setting up the level The level is attached to the tripod, and when in position the tripod legs should be spread about 750mm apart, and the parallel plates approx level. The 3rd leg of the tripod should slope away from the user to avoid him accidentally kicking or disturbing the leg.

For final levelling, the folowing operations are carried out:

The Three-Screw Level:

1. Turn the telescope until it is parallel with any two screws.
2. Hold one screw in each hand, bring the bubble of the spirit-level to the centre by adopting the following rule: turn both thumbs inwards or both outwards—the bubble always following the direction of the left thumb.
3. Having centred the bubble as above, turn the telescope 90° over the remaining screw, and centre the bubble by this screw alone.
4. Turn the telescope to the original position and check the bubble, and again over the second position.

The Four-Screw Level:

1. Turn the telescope parallel to two opposite or diagonal screws, and centre the bubble.
2. Turn the telescope 90° over the other two remaining screws and centre the bubble.
3. Check both positions again before use.
   Using the level will be described in the next Chapter.

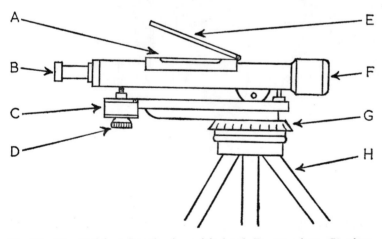

Fig 39   The Quickset Level: A—spirit level, B—eye-piece, C—circular bubble, D—tilting screw, E—mirror and spirit level cover, F—object glass, G—graduated traversing scale, H—tripod

The Quickset Level is similar to the Dumpy Level as will be seen in Fig 39, but can be more quickly adjusted and is reputed to be accurate to within 3mm in 90m.

Setting up the Level:
1. The tripod is erected as previously described and the level mounted.
2. Adjustment is made until the circular bubble is central.
3. The level is then locked by tightening the locking screw.
4. The level's telescope is sighted on the levelling staff, and set in a horizontal position.
5. The above setting is done by adjusting the tilting screw while viewing the level bubble in the mirror until it is central.
6. The reading is taken through the telescope on the levelling staff [the scale will appear inverted].

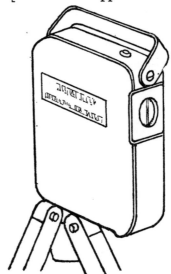

Fig 40   The Cowley level

Reading the Levelling Staff will be described in the next Chapter.

The 'Cowley' Automatic Level is a low-cost instrument for

all levelling purposes, which combines speed, is always ready for use, involves no setting-up or adjustment, and is accurate to 6mm in 30m (Fig 40). The level contains a system of mirrors which enables a horizontal 'line of sight' to be seen by looking down into an aperture on top of the instrument. A sliding staff is used with the Cowley Level, with which levels to a height or depth of 3m can be taken.

Using the Level:

1. Set up the metal tripod with the pin vertically upwards.
2. The level is mounted on to the tripod pin ensuring that the pin goes fully into the hole on the underside of the instrument.
3. An assistant is used to hold the sliding staff in a vertical position on the spot to be levelled, and with the yellow front of the staff target facing the level.
4. With the staff in position, the level user looks down into the aperture [on top of the instrument], and turns the level until the target can be seen through it and split into two halves.

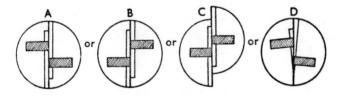

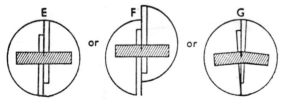

Fig 41 Viewing through the Cowley level

5. The view may appear as a whole circle as shown at A, B, or D [see Fig 41, where the target is off level], or

I

the circle may be split as shown at C—which should be ignored.

6. The reflected target may appear horizontal as at A, B, and C, or tilted as at D—which should be ignored.

7. To get the target on level, a signal is given to the assistant holding the staff to raise or lower the target on the staff until the two halves of the target are brought into coincidence as shown in Fig 41.

8. It does not matter if the two halves of the circle are level as shown at E and G or split as shown at F—the target will be level with the instrument and the height read on the Scale on the back of the Staff.

The Cowley Slope Attachment:

A 'Slope' attachment (Fig 42), can be used on the Cowley

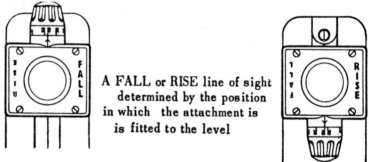

A FALL or RISE line of sight determined by the position in which the attachment is is fitted to the level

Fig 42   The Cowley slope attachment

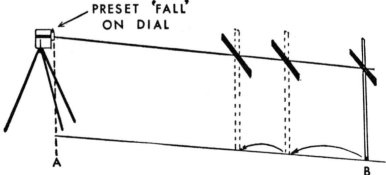

Fig 43   The use of the Cowley level where the fall or rise is known

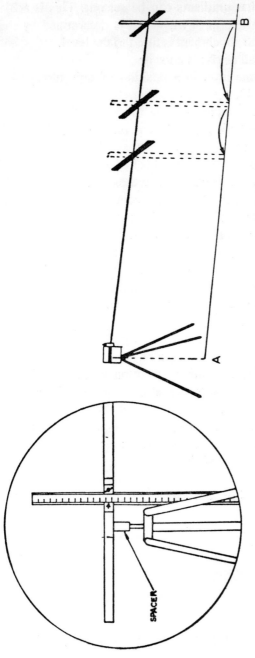

Fig 44 The use of the Cowley level where the gradient is unknown

Level so that gradients can be set out. This is achieved by a fall or rise line of sight, which is determined by the position in which the attachment is fitted to the level.

Where fall or rise is known:

1. Erect the level in a position to sight along the trench as in Fig 43.
2. Set the attachment dial to the gradient required.
3. Fit the 'Slope' attachment on the level in the fall or rise position as required.
4. Sighting through the level, the target is directed into co-incidence and clamped on the staff.
5. Move the staff to intermediate positions or pegs and adjust the heights of the latter until the target image is coincident with the line of sight.

Where the gradient is unknown:

1. Erect the tripod over point as at A in Fig 44.
2. Place the Cowley Spacer on the tripod pin.
3. Set the target on the staff as illustrated, and clamp in position.
4. Mount the level on the tripod and fit the 'slope' attachment with the dial reading zero.
5. Transfer the staff to position as at B, sight through the level, and rotate the 'slope' knob to bring the target into coincidence.
6. Move the staff to intermediate positions or pegs, adjusting the heights of some until the target image is coincident with the line of sight.

The Quick-Sight Level is a small, simple, and light weight

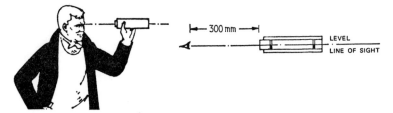

Fig 45   Using the Quick-Sight level

level, which was patented as recently as 1968. Simple to use and needing no adjustment, the level works on the principle of twin liquid levels extended with the eye to provide a level line of sight, the relative level being 'seen literally at a glance'.

Accurate to plus or minus 19mm in 30m, the level can be listed as, 'boning, cut and fill work, drainage lines, and brick

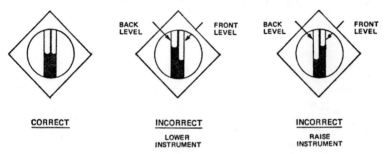

Fig 46   A level line of sight using the Quick-Sight level
Fig 47   An incorrect line of sight using the Quick-Sight level, the instrument should be lowered
Fig 48   Another incorrect line of sight with the Quick-Sight level, the
instrument should be raised

applied to all forms of levelling work, its particular uses being courses'.

Using the Level

1. The instrument is held approx 300mm from the eye, and the operator sights through the tube (Fig 45).
2. For a level line of sight, both levels must be in line with the eye as shown in Fig 46.
3. If the front tube level appears lower than the back, as seen in Fig 47, the instrument should be lowered and not the eye.
4. If the front level appears higher than the back level, as seen in Fig 48, the instrument should be raised.
5. Tilting the instrument will not bring the levels into line.
6. Besides being hand operated, the level can be held in a 'V' cut block, or a 'V'-notched rod.

19

Recording Levels

Reference has already been made to the Levelling Staff from which readings are taken after the surveyor's level has been set up. The Staffs or Staves are usually made of mahogany, with more modern types of lightweight aluminium, and they are of two main forms: (i) *Telescopic* These open up in three lengths to usual heights of 4.25m; 5m; and 6m. (ii) *Folding* A two-fold Stave with a strong hinged, or socket joint with ribbed stiffening plates and clamps which hold it in a usual extended height of from 3m to 4.25m.

Types of Levelling Staffs There are different types of levelling staffs designed and graduated according to the nature of levelling operations which have to be carried out. As many of the existing metric staves involve incorrect units of accepted measurement, the foreman should consult BS 4484, 1969, 'Specification for Measuring Instruments for Constructional Works'. The 'Watts Invar' double-divided metric reading stave is shown in Fig 49. This stave is designed for very precise levelling and it has two divided scales—the divisions at 5mm intervals are marked by lines 1mm thick.

The left-hand scale starts at the bottom of the staff, while the right-hand scale is displaced downwards. The reason for the two scales with a varying zero is to provide a check on gross errors and to increase accuracy.

Staff Markings vary in graduated form as well as the values

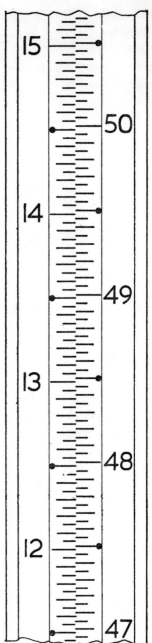

which are shown numerically. In most cases all the line markings are in black with metre number indications in red, or red and black may be used alternately for metre markings. The staff-user should acquaint himself fully with the graduations and markings and have trial readings of the staff itself before attempting to read inverted through a levelling telescope.

Levelling Terms Before dealing with the recording of levels, it is important that the foreman or building supervisor is conversant with certain terms applied, and the various 'lines of sight' which are employed. The levelling example shown in Fig 50, will help to illustrate these terms and the levels taken.

Example: Assume that a piece of undulating ground requires 6 levels to be taken between position No 1 and No 6, and that the former (No 1), is on an existing 'Bench Mark' (which is a chipped or 'v' recessed horizontal line with arrowhead below usually found in a masonry, boundary, or wall of a public building—the horizontal line indicating the height above Ordnance datum and its position being recorded on a local Ordnance Survey map).

The methods of setting up the level to take the required 6 readings would be as follows:

Fig 49   The Watts Invar metric staff

1. The level is set up at A, and readings taken on the levelling staff at positions Nos 1, 2, and 3.
2. The instrument is moved to B (set up), and a reading taken first on position No 3 (to relate the first and second stage), then readings are taken at positions Nos 4 and 5.
3. The level is then moved to C, and after setting up a reading is taken back on position No 5 before taking that at position No 6.

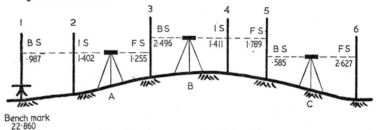

Fig 50   An example of levelling

With the above information, and reference to Fig 50, the following terms can be illustrated:

Fore Sights are the last sights to be taken before moving the instrument to a new position. Fore Sights in the example would be those at A3, B5 and C6.

Back Sights After moving the instrument to a new position, the first sight to be taken is back to the staff, which is kept in the same position where it was for the last reading before moving the level—thus these sights are known as Back Sights and in the example would be those at A1, B3 and C5.

Intermediate Sights are any number of sights taken between a Back Sight and a Fore Sight, and in the example would be those at A2 and B4.

Change Points are those at which the levelling staff is retained in position while the level is moved (so that back sights might be taken), these in the example being at positions 3 and 5.

Reduced Level at any position or point, is its vertical height above a Datum Line [which may be a selected one or the Ordnance Datum]. In the example, the first sight at position No 1 gives a staff reading of 0.987m above a Bench Mark, which is 75ft or 22.860m above Ordnance Datum.

The Height of Collimation at position No 1, would therefore be 22.860m plus 0.987m, which equals 23.847m above Ordnance Datum.

The Staff reading at position No 2, is 1.402m.

Therefore the Reduced Level at position No 2 would be 23.847 minus 1.402, which equals 22.445m AOD [above Ordnance Datum].

Feet and Conversion to Metres In time all the Ordnance Survey maps will be metricated with the heights above sea level given in metres. Until this is completed, it may be necessary to take levels from the map given in feet and translate them into metres. This is done by multiplying the feet dimensions by the conversion factor of 0.3048, thus the Bench Mark figure of 75ft in the example would be 75 multiplied by 0.3048—giving 22.860m.

An Instant Conversion aluminium alloy Stave is available with Cowley Automatic Levels, which will give an English Feet reading of from nought to 6ft 6in, with the equivalent in metric.

Simple Levelling is the term applied when all the levels needed can be obtained from one position or a single setting up of the level.

Compound Levelling is when the number of levels required makes it necessary to move the level to different positions [as in the example].

Booking of Staff Readings The system of booking or recording the level readings is done by one of two methods: The Rise and Fall Method, and The Height of Collimation Method.

Examples of readings are shown on the part Metric Levelling Staff face shown in Fig. 51. The millimetre readings (of up to four figures), which will dispense with a decimal marker, are recorded according to the type of level they are

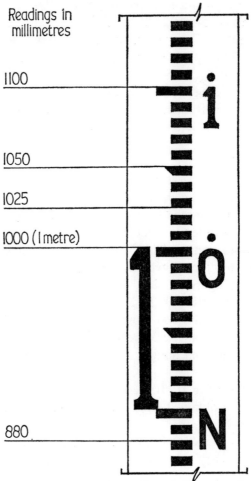

Readings in
millimetres

1100

1050

1025

1000 (1 metre)

880

Fig 51   Part of a metric levelling staff with readings

in their appropriate columns (eg back sight, fore sight etc).

Where reduced levels are linked to an Ordnance Datum and the readings are given in metres, a decimal marker is re-quired but their use is confined to the reduced level column. The various sight levels used in the example are recorded in the two methods of booking to illustrate the booking system.

Readings at a Change Point Both the readings (back sight

and fore sight), taken at a change point have the same reduced
level and are both recorded on the same line.

Back Sight	Inter. Sight	Fore Sight	Rise	Fall	Reduced Level	Position or Distance	Remarks
0.987					22.860m	0	Bench Mark
	1.402			0.415	22.445		
2.496		1.255	0.147		22.592		Change Point
	1.411		1.085		23.677		
0.585		1.789		0.378	23.299		Change Point
		2.627		2.042	21.257		
4.068		5.671	1.232	2.835			
		4.068		1.232			
		1.603	Fall	1.603	Fall		

Fig 52   The Rise and Fall method

The Rise and Fall Method gives a mathematical check
when comparison is made between the difference in the sum
of the back sights and fore sights, with a difference in the sum
of the rises and falls. The above check figure should also
equal the difference between the highest and lowest reduced
levels.

The main feature of the Height of Collimation Method, is
the calculating of the Height of Collimation for every position
in which the level is used. The Height of Collimation at position No 1, will be 22.860m plus the first back sight reading
of 0.987, which will equal 23.847m above the Ordnance
Datum. The reduced level at any position is obtained by sub-
tracting the level reading from the appropriate Height of
Collimation, thus the reduced level of position No 2, will be
1.402 subtracted from 23.847 thus giving 22.445m. At a
Change Point, if the reduced level is added to the back sight

Back Sight	Inter. Sight	Fore Sight	Height of Colli- mation	Reduced Level	Position or Distance	Remarks
0.987			23.847	22.860m	0	Bench Mark
	1.402			22.445		
2.496		1.255	25.088	22.592		Change Point
	1.411			23.677		
0.585		1.789	23.884	23.299		Change Point
		2.627		21.257		
4.068		5.671		22.860		
		4.068		21.257		
		1.603	Fall	1.603	Fall	

Fig 53   The Height of Collimation method

—then the new Height of Collimation is obtained. Thus the Height of Collimation at the level position 'C' in the example will be 23.299 plus the back sight reading of 0.585—thus giving 23.884m.

20

Existing Buildings

WORK ON FAULTS, FAILURES, EQUIPMENT, SAFEGUARDS AND PROTECTION

Diagnosis of Faults and Failures Investigate fully any faults and determine if they are superficial or structural. If superficial consider any weakness which may ensue in carrying out the repairs (eg exposure of water pipes, opening of drains, exposure of live cable etc). If structural, decide on the extent of the work in relation to the safety of the building or adjoining property. Determine the trades and operations needed for the work, as a craft foreman may inspect a job to find that other trades may be required before his own. Look for the cause of the fault—age of building, poor materials, weather, drainage, subsidence, deliberate damage, or nuisance from adjoining properties (tree roots, drains etc).

Treatment Where work entails excavations or demolitions etc, the foreman should acquaint himself with The Construction, (General Provisions) Regulations, 1961. Unless in an emergency, consideration should be given to the time of the year in relation to the work being done (cold or damp, exposure, or dirty conditions). Consider any safety requirements to owner's property, or to adjacent property before commencing work (see later notes in this Chapter). Plan the work and the possible sequence of trades carefully, and the use of any plant which may cause damage or danger (such as excavations etc).

141

Organisation and Supervision of Repairs Make a careful selection of competent men for the job in hand (a competent man for repairs might be selected not on his ability as a craftsman, but on being a clean and tidy worker and being able to get on well with clients). Plan carefully the requirements of men, materials and plant to avoid the risk of delays or loss of time. The suitability of the job and size of site may restrict the number of men or disposition of materials.

Time planning may have to be reviewed daily due to snags or unforeseen contingences arising. On restricted jobs, try to visit and inspect the work daily (if not permanently on the job), in order to plan further stages of work or requisition of materials.

Ensure that a careful survey is made of repair work for estimating purposes, as unforeseen operations or omissions may lead to a loss on the job. Keep careful records of materials and time, especially if the job is to be charged as daywork.

Alterations and Extensions Check on planning permission having been obtained from the local authority, as this may have been sought by the client. Also check (where appropriate), the distance between buildings and the possibility of 'Ancient Lights'.

Ensure that extensions do not encroach beyond the 'Building Line' of the property, or 'Improvement Line' where this may have been given by the local authority. Check carefully on levels, particularly floor levels on sloping sites where floors may have to be extended.

For extensions, check on service requirements, eg will further electrical work overload a circuit; or boilers, cisterns, and storage tanks be adequate to deal with extended installations. Check on existing drains where waste pipes have to be installed, or to prevent their covering by accident, and check on the possible diversion of service mains (gas, water, and electricity), which in the process of building work might be covered over. Check on any encroachment to neighbours' properties, or permission required from neighbours to uncover any drains or services etc.

Special Equipment for Repair Work It is difficult to generalise as to what special equipment might be required in repair work, as this would depend on the type of work and its magnitude, and the trades involved.

Where power tools are to be used, ensure the use of a transformer and not risk main voltage which might be available and handy. Site any noisy plant, if possible, away from the occupied parts of the building. Any plant or cables should be placed or sited so as not to endanger occupants, with special care where there are children about.

Nomination of specialist firms should be made where the work involves such things as: Piling, Pressure Piling, Pressure Concrete, Inserted Damp Courses, Site De-watering, or Demolitions etc.

Protection of Private Owners The work, repairs, or alterations should be done to coincide with the client's convenience of time. Where much inconvenience may be caused by repairs and alterations, the work should be geared to cut down the time factor—this may entail overtime work.

Where materials or opening of services may restrict entrances etc, consider the covering of drives and possible use of duckboards, handrails, small bridges, or temporary stairs. This would also apply to the general public. Use temporary coverings where doors, windows, or walls may be exposed; or windbreaks in bad weather. Try to limit any inconvenience caused by cuts in services, respecting the requirements of the client.

Protection of General Public On sites of special interest, or where there is likely to be congestion of the public, consider the provision of observation panels.

Use Gantries with hoods if the work is overhead over public thoroughfares and consider the following:
(i) Use of tarpaulins if the work entails cleaning down; (ii)

lighting between sunset and sunrise if the gantry obstructs part of a thoroughfare; (iii) provision of a temporary footpath and handrail if encroachment is made on a roadway; (iv) where encroachment is made on a roadway, a wooden kerb must be provided to protect the gantry from traffic; (v) obtain permission for part or full closure to public of a thoroughfare from the local authority; (vi) display the notice on site granting permission from the local authority to close the thoroughfare; and (vi) where delivery of materials or plant may interfere with the general public or traffic, notify the police in advance and get their advice and help.

Precautions to Safeguard Adjoining Properties Properties and adjoining properties are more likely to need safeguards from the following: excavations, demolitions, falling materials and danger of collapse etc. The first two situations are covered by the Construction (General Provisions) Regulations, 1961, and the main safeguards are outlined below with reference to the regulation concerned:

Excavation No excavation or earthwork should be carried out which is likely to endanger the stability of any structure or person employed. Fencing of excavations should be carried out with a suitable barrier to a height of at least 600mm, and as close as is practicable to the edge where any fall would be more than a vertical distance of 1.95m. Safeguarding the edges of excavations shall be made by not placing materials or loads so near as to cause collapse and thereby endanger any person.

No person shall be employed in any part of an excavation unless that part has been inspected that day by a competent person, (GP 9.1). The effect of climatic conditions involving rain and frost on excavations should be appreciated, (GP 10.3).

Demolitions (*in whole or part*) should be supervised by a competent person experienced in demolition, and the sequence of work planned beforehand (GP 39.1). Before demolition, no electric cable liable to be a source of danger shall remain charged, (GP 44.1). Prevent danger from risk of fire, or explosion through leakage of gas or vapour, (GP 40. a.). Prevent risk of flooding from water mains, sewers, or culverts, (GP 40. b.). No roof or floor should be overloaded with debris so as to make it unsafe, (GP 46.1.).

The following operations shall be carried out only under immediate supervision of a competent foreman or charge-hand, or by workmen experienced in this kind of work and under direction as aforesaid:

(i) Demolition of framework, or any roof, floor, wall, staircase, or chimney, except where there is no risk of collapse or a risk that could not reasonably have been foreseen; (ii) actual demolition of any part of a building where there is a special risk of collapse; and (iii) the cutting of reinforced concrete, steelwork, or ironwork forming part of the structure.

Shoring Before demolition is commenced and also during the progress of the work, precautions shall where necessary be taken by adequate shoring or otherwise to prevent as far as practicable, the accidental collapse of any part of the building or any adjoining building, the collapse of which may endanger any person employed.

Protection from Falling Materials Any place on site where a person is habitually employed shall be covered to protect any person from being struck by falling material or article. Scaffold materials, tools, objects, or materials including waste must not be thrown, tipped, or shot down from a height liable to cause injury, but properly lowered. Where lowering is not practicable and where any part of a structure is being demolished or broken off, steps shall be taken where necessary to protect persons employed from falling or flying debris.

Avoidance of Danger from Collapse of a Structure All practical precautions shall be taken by the use of temporary

K

supports and fixings to prevent danger through collapse during any temporary state of weakness. Any work carried out likely to reduce so as to endanger any person employed, or stability of the building during construction, all precautions shall be taken by shoring or otherwise to prevent danger from collapse or fall of any part thereof.

PART THREE

RECORDS

21

The Site Office

The foreman as an administrator must have some form of office provision, but this depends on the size of the job or the number of operatives under his control. Although The Offices, Shops, and Railway Premises Act, 1963, does not apply to building sites, it does apply to builders' site offices and staff canteens.

The following site offices would be excluded from the Act: (i) those where only self-employed people or close relatives of the employer work; (ii) those where the total hours worked are normally not more than 21 each week; (iii) mobile offices set in one place for a period not exceeding 6 months.

Site Office Requirements All offices not excluded from the Act, must be notified to HM Inspector of Factories, and must conform to the following:

1. Cleanliness—Floors and steps must be cleaned at least once a week and the premises otherwise kept clean.
2. Overcrowding—Forty square feet of floor space, (but not less than 400 cubic feet), for each person.
3. Temperature—Approved methods of heating must be provided for the premises to attain a temperature of at least 60.8 degrees Fahrenheit within one hour of starting time. A thermometer must be provided.
4. Ventilation must be effective.
5. Lighting must be adequate.

6. Other requirements relate to sanitation, washing, seats, first aid, fire and accidents occurring.

Although the above may seem irrelevant to the meagre provision which is more commonly found, it could well be that on large sites better provision is made and where there are good site offices, the craft foreman might share such luxury, and therefore should be acquainted with the Act requirements. Under less favourable provision, the foreman should still aim for the ideal even though this may entail some improvisation.

Minimum Office Requirements A hut, cabin, or room of a building, which could be utilised as an office, and contain the job's relevant plans and drawings with provision for storing same (either cabinet, wall-mounting, or flat display). There must be provision for letters, orders, and variations, files for delivery notes and records [see later reference], first aid box or requirements. Any regulations or posters which apply to a particular craft, and stationery and order books, according to the systems used by the firm or demanded by the job, must be available here, and a thermometer, especially for the trowel trades. Some form of washing facilities in order to clean-up for clerical work must be provided, and tape, square, measuring or setting out and levelling instruments which apply to the trade.

TIME SHEETS

Accurate time-keeping is the basis of ascertaining labour costs, and production can only be fully operational if each operative's time is accounted for. Time sheets are normally of two types: daily, where jobbing, day-work, or component work for varying contracts is being done, and weekly, suitable for repetition work or site work on contract. The weekly sheet usually operates with the first day being that after wages are made up, eg if wages are paid on a Friday, the week would no doubt end on a Wednesday or Thursday.

Time Sheet Preparation can be something of a tradition,

(To be used ONLY for a Group of Workers employed on
                     Similar Work)

Day .... Job or Site .... Sheet No ....

Date ....19.....   Trade ....

Operative	Hours	Over Time	Deduction Late Start	Total Hours	Rate
Totals:					

Signed: .... Charge Hand

Checked .... Foreman

Abstracted .... Costing Clerk

Fig 54 A daily group time sheet

which follows a set method or policy of a firm. Preparation
can be adapted for the sheet to be held on the site, or held by
the firm's office. If held on the site [see later notes on
analysis], the foreman may have to compile and submit a
Payroll or Wages Sheet to the firm's office for payment of
wages. Site-held sheets need only contain reference to work
done and hours worked.

If the sheets are to be held by the office and are one of a weekly type, they could include appropriate columns for office use relating to rate, overtime hours, deductions, travelling time, and allowances etc.

All time sheets should include reference to time and materials for work relating to variations or extras to contract.

Name of Site or Job No .... Week Ending .... Sheet No																		
NAME	Thursday Overtime	FRIDAY	SATURDAY	SUNDAY	MONDAY	TUESDAY	WEDNESDAY	THURSDAY	Time Payable	TOTAL HOURS	RATE	Wage Total	Wages Transfer	Fares/Allowance	Gross Wages	Income Tax Deduct.	Firm / Men Insurance	NET WAGES
											£	£	£	£	£	£	£ £	£

Fig 55 A wages sheet which could be adjusted to suit a firm's particular requirements with columns added to include tool money or holiday pay etc

All time sheets for jobbing or day-work should include provision for materials used to be recorded.

Analysis of Sheets Apart from the firm's policy, the foreman should decide on the vital information required for the

Name A. Green		Trade Carpenter & Joiner		Week Ending May 1st	
Day	Contract or Job	Work Done	Machine Time (Hr)	Normal Time (Hr)
Thursday	Timber Daywork (Smith)	Unloading/Stacking Panelled Doors	2½	2 3½
Friday	Black Cat Cafe Daywork (Smith)	Frames & Sashes Doors & Sanding	4	2½ 1½
Monday	Daywork (Smith) Primary School	Cupboard Doors Shelves	2½ 1½	2½ 1½
Tuesday	Primary School Oaklawn Hospital	Prep. Skirting Oak Door & Frame	2 1	2 3
Wednesday	Hospital	Prep. Skirting Oak Door & Frame	2	6
	Total		15½	24½

Summary:- (Allocation in Hours)

Contract or Job	Machine Time	Normal Time
Timber Daywork (Smith's Shop) Black Cat Cafe Primary School Oaklawn Hospital	5 4 3½ 3	2 7½ 2½ 3½ 9
	15½	24½

Fig 56   A weekly time sheet

execution of his duties. He should ensure that all employees including apprentices are conversant with the job reference, or number, or site name [to coincide with contract or order]. Information should be given on the compiling of the sheets, and the means of deposit or collection on completion. To help in the analysis of work, uniformity in operations or stage work must be made clear, eg 1st or 2nd fixings, or 1st lift etc. Where petty cash is claimed for the purchase of materials or fittings, the cash receipt should be tendered with the time sheet.

Where the job analysis or costing is done fully by the firm's office, then the foreman need only check the hours worked, but should also extract for his own information and for diary entry the dates of work being done on extras, variations, or deviations from the contract. Where site costing or time pro-

gramming is essential, and becomes the foreman's responsibility, then the greatest care in compiling and analysis must
be followed by an accurate filing system.

Filing of time sheets can be done under Daily, Weekly, or
Job headings as required. If essential for labour costing, sub-
divisions of the sheets could be made for craftsmen, apprentices, and labourers. Where staging costs are required, or the
time factors for various stages of work—then filing can be
done under stages such as 1st lift Brickwork, 2nd Floor Car-
cassing etc. Where time is split on a weekly time sheet between
jobs or stages, then the extracted information may be recorded on Job or Staging record cards or sheets. If provision
is made on the Programme Chart, with adequate space, then
hours of work done can be recorded against hours of work
programmed.

22

Daywork and Variations

RECORDS AND ACCOUNTS

The RIBA Form of Contract states, 'Where work cannot be properly measured and valued, the Contractor shall be allowed daywork rates on the prices prevailing when such work is carried out'. The questions on decisions being made as to whether work shall be carried out under daywork charges, will usually be made by the quantity surveyor, if he considers that the work or circumstances under which it has to be carried out justifies a daywork claim.

Vouchers for daywork shall be sent to the architect, or his representative, for checking and verification not later than the end of the week following that in which the work was done.

Types of jobs justifying daywork include work which the quantity surveyor cannot estimate accurately—such as pumping water, underpinning, filling of craters, and possible site clearance; manual work in restricted situations or encroachments, where normal methods or use of mechanical plant would not be possible; provision of openings, chasings or channels [for doors, windows, service pipes, or drains], in walls or floors after completion; and any variation to the contract which may be required by the client or architect.

Attendance on Other Trades Extra work which is done in attendance on other trades, or for sub-contractors, or special-

155

D. Brown & Son, Ltd, Newhomes Estate, Newtown.

Extra Work Account

Job or Contract ...Queens Hotel......   Week Ending ...May 12th............

Description of Work Done	Trade	Hours	Materials Used
Cutting and recessing joists for conduit for Electrical Contractor	C & J	3	
Cutting holes in walls for soap and toilet roll holder provided by client, and making good	Brick,	2	
Cutting holes for air bricks and forming new path level.	Brick. Labor.	8 8	Three 225mm x 150mm air-bricks. Six 600mm x 600mm paving slabs.

Fig 57   An extra work account sheet

ists, other than the normal type of service which would be allowed for under the terms of 'waiting on other trades', in the contract, would justify daywork charges being made.

Recording of Daywork

Records must be kept on a weekly basis because of the weekly vouchers required by the architect. A check should be made on the firm's method of submitting the vouchers— normally the craft foreman to general foreman or to the head office by a certain day of the week. The foreman must record the number of hours worked, the materials used, and the use of any plant or plant hire, for the duration of the job.

The foreman must ensure, as has been previously emphasised, that the recording of daywork on operatives' time sheets is accurately done. For easy recording or reference, the foreman may consider separate daily or weekly time sheets being used specially for daywork. Unless the foreman has a good system of recording the materials used, which may be difficult on a large site, the workmen should be instructed to record an accurate statement of materials used in making out their time sheets. An accurate recording of materials used is essential, as this item, more than hours worked, will obviously be closely checked by the quantity surveyor.

Daywork Accounts Normally the account would be rendered by the firm's office and the foreman would have no

Daily Timesheet for Jobbing or Daywork					
Job or Contract		Client or Job No. ....Transport Cafe....			
Day & Date ....Mon May 8th..........		Workman & Trade ....C. Smith. C&J.			
(Record Materials used on the reverse side of Form)					
Job or Site Transferred From	Description of Work	Time		For Office Use	
		Hr	Min	Rate	£
Spent first hour at Queens Hotel	New sash cord, repairs to door, and making good prior to painting	7	0		
Signed Client: ....H. Davies............... (Correct Hours Worked & Service)					
Signed: Foreman or Chargehand: ....J. Jones................ (Foreman)					

Fig 58   A daily time sheet for jobbing or daywork

action in compiling of same. The amount of wages charged, may include basic wages, bonus, overtime, travelling allowances, subsistence, and time lost due to bad weather, and a record of such should be included or recorded with the daywork records.

Methods of ordering materials, components and plant Materials etc can be ordered from one of two sources: Suppliers, manufacturers, or merchants [by order]; and from stores or stock [by requisition].

Order books should be in triplicate, with pages of distinct colour for easy reference. (i) Original copy is sent to the supplier; (ii) the second copy [according to firm's policy], is given

Messrs Smith & Jones, *(Architects & Surveyors),*
Castle Buildings,
Castle Street,
Newtown.

1st April 1971

Variation Order No: ......3.(three)....................

Contract: ..New Residence – "The Retreat"....

M ....D. Brown & Son, Ltd, Builders,.............. are hereby authorised,

according to the conditions of the Form of Contract, (as above), to

perform the following work, viz.:-

1. Carry out the necessary construction and fixing of the Aluminium
   Picture Window to Lounge, in accordance with Drawing No 21.

2. Cut new window opening in west exterior wall of Hall, for provision
   of Bull's Eye Window, as directed on site, (29/3/71).

3. Omit the concrete coping to the Yard boundary wall.

4. Substitute a Brickette Fireplace, (chosen by client), instead of the
   tiled one specified, at a total extra cost of £20.

(Signed) A. Smith, A I R B A,
Architect.

Fig 59   A variation order

to the firm's storekeeper, or to head office with the delivery
note; and (iii) the third copy is retained in the order book.

Where goods are ordered for daywork or extras, details
should be stated on the order or counterfoil so that it can be
recorded on the invoice later, such information being of great
value when making up the final account.

When an order is given verbally, or by phone, it should be confirmed by order form and care should be taken to state it is confirmation only. This will prevent the order being duplicated.

(Goods Supplied without a printed Order will not be allowed in the Account)

FROM: D. Brown, Builder,   NO: 683
        New House Estate,
        Newtown.   DATE: May 1st, 1971

TO: Cement Depot,
        Industrial Estate,
        Newtown.

Please Deliver To: ....Builders Yard............. as early as possible:

    10 tonnes of Cement at £10 per tonne as quoted.
    Confirming telephone message today (Red Ink)

Account: (General Stores)   Signed on behalf of
                                        D. Brown

                                   ..C. Smith, Foreman..

Fig 60   A page from an order book

Store requisition book, when ordering goods or materials from the firm's store, yard, or workshop, the order should be made by the foreman in triplicate as follows: (i) the original and second copies are sent to the storekeeper when goods are required or issued; (ii) the third copy remains in the requisition book; and (iii) after issue of goods and receipt of signature for same, the original copy will be forwarded to head office, and the second copy held by the storekeeper.

Deliveries of materials When delivery or advice notes are received, they should be attached to the order copy [if on site] or store copy if materials are being taken into stock.

(Requisition Form for Materials, Plant or Equipment, on Stores)

Trade .... Date 19

Contract or Job	Tally or Store no	Description of Materials	Stores Issued	Price £ p	Remarks

Person Ordering: Debit to Stores Stock:

SIGNATURE .... STOREKEEPER

Person Receiving: Adjusted in Cost Record Ledger

SIGNATURE .... OFFICE/CLERK

DATE 19

Note:-   If the Quantity detailed is not Received, amend the figures in Red Ink to agree with the Actual amount Received.

Fig 61   A requisition of stores

Any differences in amounts etc of materials ordered and those received should be dealt with immediately. Deliveries should be checked for breakages or shortages, if possible before unloading. When damaged goods are accepted and delivered, the driver's attention should be drawn to same and his delivery note adjusted and signed accordingly. Any such goods, except where the supplier's or manufacturer's own transport is used and would return same, should be put in a safe place as evidence pending inquiries which may be made

Weekly Account of Materials Delivered

Site or Job: Queens Hotel   Week Ending .... May 4th ....

Date	Loads	Materials	Amount	Ticket Number	Received From	Carrier
April 30th	3	Bricks	1,500		Hospital Site	R. James
May 1st	12	Stone Ballast	20 tonnes		Cafe Site	Own Lorry
	1	Bags of Cement	20	3456	British Rail	Own Lorry
	1	Ballast	1 tonne	6543	BR Service	Own Lorry
	2	Mortar			Yard	Own Lorry
May 2nd	2	Walling Stone	9 tonnes	999	British Rail	R. James
	2	Sand	8 tonnes	6789	BR Service	R. James

All Materials returned to Yard or sent to another Site must be recorded on the reverse side of this sheet.

Fig 62   A weekly account of materials delivered

L

Weekly Account of Supply & Return of Plant, Equipment, Tools					
Site or Job ..... Transport Cafe			Week Ending .... May 12th		
Date Received	Ticket Number	Plant/Equipment	Received From	Date Removed	Forwarded To
May 7th	123	20 Scaffold Boards 12 Base Plates 12 Joint Pins 10 Putlogs 20 Double Couplers	Yard	End of Month	Queens Hotel
May 8th	456	Extension Ladder 6 Picks 6 Spades 2 Barrows 3 Mortar Boards			
May 9th	789	6 Ranging Rods 8 Road Lamps 4 Trestles	Queens Hotel	May 7th	Firswood School

Fig 63   A weekly account of the supply and return of plant

in respect of any claim. The custom of signing for goods delivered as 'not examined', is now treated by many carriers as a clear signature, and no claim for shortages or damage will be entertained unless the items are stated on the delivery notes.

Claims when there is a case for a claim, an invoice should be rendered to the suppliers as soon as possible stating: (i) the amount of damage suffered including if appropriate, the actual cost of replacement; (ii) the time and date that the goods were received; (iii) the carrier's name and any reference which may appear on the delivery note or sheet; and (iv) the firm or claimant's full address.

23

Stock Checking
and Site Meetings

Under terms of most contracts, the main contractor is required to provide adequate storage for the sub-contractors' materials, and these goods must also be accommodated in lockable stores. This is mentioned because the foreman may be concerned with a sub-contract trade.

PERIODICAL STOCK CHECKS

Stock checks are essential in order that the total material requirements for any job can be compared against: (i) those materials already used or in use; (ii) the quantity in stock; and (iii) the materials outstanding from suppliers, or those possibly rejected which require replacement.

Stock Checks Show: (i) stock quantity plus materials outstanding from suppliers should be sufficient to complete the job; (ii) materials delivered, less the materials on stock, gives the materials used; and (iii) the total materials [from the Bill of Quantities], less the materials on stock and undelivered, gives the materials used.

Stock Control According to the trade and the size or value of the job, the materials may be kept on site or in the builder's yard. For a large builder's yard, and if the number and quality of materials demand it, it is likely that a storekeeper or similar employee will be engaged. The foreman is more directly concerned with the stocks only on a job under his control.

Some trades will have a high wastage [bricks, cement, plaster etc] as opposed to other trades which rely on fittings or fixtures.

The foreman must decide on one of two methods of controlling stocks according to his trade and requirements; (i) requisition against contract commitment, bearing in mind the wastage and delivery factors; (ii) by fixing maximum and minimum stock figures to hold for each type of material, and when the stocks fall to the minimum figure, making an order of a sufficient quantity to bring the stock back to maximum.

The second method above, is useful where large quantities of materials are needed daily over long periods, such as those required for the trowel trades (sand, lime, cement, bricks, plaster etc).

Date Received	Advice Note No	Supplier	Description	Tally Card No	Empties Etc	Remarks
28/3/71	PA 99	B. Jones & Co	20 No 900mm x 450mm 6mm thick Plate Glass (Clear) 12 No 600mm x 450mm 6mm thick Wired Plate Glass (Clear)	GL/9 GL/6	1 No Crate	Marked BJ 99 Returnable

Fig 64   A page from a material store ledger

Materials stored and stock checks On delivery, all goods should be recorded in a Materials Store Ledger Fig 64. The goods are then recorded on Tally Cards, according to the type, pattern, or size etc Fig 65. On requisition or use, the

Name or Description ...Sawn Softwood........................... Stock or Storage Ref No ....Shop...
Size or No ......100 x 50 (Joinery)..............................

RECEIVED				ISSUED			
Order No	Date	Supplier	Qty.	Date	Req. No	Job or Site Allocation	Quantity
A/101	1/3/71	S. Brown Ltd	1,000M	20/3- 25/3	123 234	Church Roof New Estate	500M 100M
	1/4/71	Stock Check:	Tally Card and Stock Agree, Signed			J. Smith................... Foreman	......
	1/4/71	In Stock	40M				

Fig 65   A tally card

Date	Invoice No	Name & Address	No	Size	Des. or Marks	Price	Date Ret.	Advice No	Credit No	Remarks
28/3	PA 99	B. Jones & Co	1	4M X 1M X 1M W	BJ 99	£0.50	29/3	567	678	

Fig 66 A page from the empties book

issue is recorded on the Tally Card. For any one material, on making a Stock Check, the total allocated subtracted from the total supplied, should equal the amount in stock.

Empties Book Many materials or components are delivered in crates, which are chargeable unless returned within a given period. A record of all empty crates, drums, or sacks, should be entered in the Empties Book [Fig 66] in the order in which they appear in the Store Ledger, and the same applies to credit notes received for empties returned.

Return of materials to stock Where materials have been requisitioned and booked out to a site and are not used, these are returned to stock and a credit note issued for same, which helps the stock records to be corrected.

LOCAL AUTHORITY NOTICE

Details are given in Schedule 2, Regulation A9, of the Building Regulations, outlining the 'Giving of Notices and Deposit of Plans', which are required by a local authority in relation to building work. Basically, the Notices required are as follows: (i) notice of intention to build; (ii) notice of commencement of work or stages; and (iii) notice of completion of work or stages.

Notice of Intention to Build Any person who intends to erect, make structural alterations, or extensions to a building,

COUNTY BOROUGH

Building Regulations 1965

Omitting or neglecting to give this notice before commencing the Excavations, Erection, or Alteration of any Building, renders the Owner liable to a penalty of £100. Public Health Act 1961. Section 4.

Notice required to be given under Regulation A10.

.................................196......

To The BOROUGH ENGINEER & PLANNING OFFICER

No. of Plan ....

Sir,

I hereby give you 24 hours' notice from the date of

receipt hereof that I shall commence the ....

in ....

for Mr. ....

on the expiration of this notice, plans for which were

approved by the Council on ....

Signed ....
Owner, Agent, Architect or Builder

FOR OFFICIAL USE ONLY

This Notice was received on .... the

.... *day of* ....196...

Signed ....

Date of Inspection ....

COUNTY BOROUGH

Building Regulations 1965

Omitting or neglecting to give this notice before covering up any SEWER or DRAIN, or any FOUNDATION, SITE COVERING or DAMP COURSE of a Building, renders the Owner liable to a penalty of £100. Public Health Act, 1961. Section 4.

Notice required to be given under Regulation A10

.................................196......

To The BOROUGH ENGINEER & PLANNING OFFICER

No. of Plan ....

Sir,

I hereby give you 24 hours' notice from the date of

receipt hereof that the

    (1) ....

at   (2) ....

in   (3) ....

for   (4) ....

is ready for inspection.

Signed ....
Owner, Agent, Architect or Builder.

(1) here insert 'excavation for foundation', 'sewer', 'drain', ('foundation', 'damp course'), 'site coveting'),
(2) here insert situation of premises.
(3) here insert name of road.
(4) here insert name of owner.

FOR OFFICIAL USE ONLY

This Notice was received at .... *on the*

.... *day of* ....196.....

Examined at .... *on the* ....

day of .... 196... *Signed* ....

COUNTY BOROUGH

Building Regulations 1965

Omitting or neglecting to give this notice seven clear days before occupying or completing ANY DWELLING HOUSE or after completing ANY OTHER BUILDING renders the Owner liable to a penalty of £100. Public Health Act, 1961. Section 4.

Notice required to be given under Regulation A10

.................................196...

To The BOROUGH ENGINEER & PLANNING OFFICER.

No. of Plan ....

Sir,

I hereby give you seven days' notice that the whole of

the works for the erection of...........................

in ....

for Mr. ....

have been completed and are ready for occupation.

Signed ....
Owner, Agent, Architect or Builder.

FOR OFFICIAL USE ONLY

This Notice was received on ....*the*

.... *day of* ....196..

Signed ....

Date of Inspection ....

Fig 67   Local Authority notices to commence, inspect, and completion of work

or make any material change, or install any fittings, shall [if the Regulations apply to such operations] give notices and deposit plans, sections, specifications, and written particulars, to the Local Authority.

Notice of Commencement of Certain Stages of Work (Reg A10). [Note the expression '24 hours' notice', shall not include a Saturday, Sunday, Christmas Day, Good Friday, bank holiday, or day appointed for public thanksgiving or mourning]:
(a) Not less than 24 hours' notice in writing of the date and time at which the operation will be commenced.
(b) Not less than 24 hours' notice in writing before the covering up of any excavation for a foundation, any foundation, any damp-proof course, or any concrete or other material laid over a site.
(c) Not less than 24 hours' notice in writing before any private drain or sewer [to which the Regulations apply], will be haunched or covered in any way.
(d) Notice in writing not more than 7 days after the work of laying such drain or private sewer has been carried out, including any necessary work of haunching or surrounding the drain or sewer with concrete and back-filling the trench.

Note of Completion The builder shall give to the Local Authority notice in writing of:
(a) The erection of a building not more than 7 days after completion, or [if a building or part is occupied before completion], not less than 7 days before occupation as well as not more than 7 days after completion.
(b) Any alteration or extension of a building, not more than 7 days after completion.
(c) The execution of works or the installation of fittings in connection with a building, not more than 7 days after completion.

Giving of Notices and Deposit of Plans The following

general provisions are given under Schedule 2, of The Building Regulations, 1965; SI 1965 No 1373:

1. Notices and other particulars shall be given in writing.
2. Drawings shall be executed or reproduced in a clear and intelligible manner with suitable and durable materials. Plans and sections shall be to a scale of not less than 1:100 (10mm to 1m) or, if the building is so extensive as to render a smaller scale necessary not less than 1:200 (5mm to 1m); block plans shall be to a scale of not less than 1/250; and key plans shall be to a scale of not less than 1/2500.
   The scale shall be indicated on all plans, sections and other drawings and the north point on all block plans and key plans.
3. Every notice, drawing or other document shall be signed by the person required to furnish it to the local authority or by his duly-authorised agent, and if it is signed by such agent it shall state the name and address of the person on whose behalf it has been furnished.
4. Every such document, together with a duplicate thereof, shall be sent or delivered to the offices of the local authority.

Note: As the Building Regulations, 1965, gave drawing scales which were in the foot-inch system, these have been adapted above to the nearest metric system which is at present [at the time of compiling] accepted by local authorities.

SITE MEETINGS

Site meetings are held so that progress and planning can be controlled throughout any contract. These meetings, according to their nature, those attending, and the type of work involved, can be known under other names, such as staff meetings, joint consultative meetings, works councils, and joint production committees etc.

Any meetings defined as site meetings or otherwise, can be called at any time by the architect, clerk of works, site agent, general foreman, or craft foreman, according to the nature or importance of items which are to be discussed.

On large sites or contracts, a monthly meeting would be called with the following members present: architect, site agent, general foreman, contracts manager, site engineer, and possibly quantity surveyor, along with the specialist or sub-contracting foremen, according to the nature of the job.

If there is a local architect, it is likely he would pay a weekly visit, otherwise the weekly meeting called at the end of the week to discuss the following week's progress, would involve the site agent, general foreman, craft foremen, specialist or sub-contracting foremen, and consultants and administration personnel as required.

Object of Site Meetings (i) Enables suggestions or expressions of views to be made; (ii) solutions found to problems, and a promotion of team spirit; (iii) permits joint discussion between all trades or groups; (iv) helps to improve efficiency through the co-operative effort which is promoted; and (v) provides an effective method of reaching and maintaining good industrial relations.

Craft site meetings would enable information to be passed quickly, and the foreman can feel reactions or impressions; enable joint discussion to be made on bonus or incentive schemes, or methods of measuring same; permit discussion dealing with social or recreational activities, or aid to fellow operatives in time of need.

The meetings should not be allowed to become dictatorial, or purely a get-together where demands, concessions, or the like are the only things discussed.

The foreman and site meetings Where the craft foreman attends a site meeting as representative of his craft, he must express views and opinions which are in the interests of his craft, and which will be in accordance with his firm's policy and help to promote progress or productivity. He should attempt to gain as much information as possible from such meetings so that this may be passed on to his operatives, appropriate, as a well informed team will be much more co-operative if they are taken into confidence about the job as a whole.

A Craft Site Meeting The craft foreman should, in relation to a craft meeting give plenty of notice, if possible, to all operatives of the time and place of the meeting; have an agenda, and take notes or minutes; try to employ democratic rules in order the prevent the ardent trade unionist [without being unkind], or the gifted worker-orator from monopolising the meeting; and try to make the line of thought constructive, and not destructive, especially if trade practice is at stake.

The more the foreman makes this sort of meeting seem important and serious, the more serious will it be absorbed by the operatives.

24

Further Records

Although paper work or administration is something of a nuisance, certain records are indispensable, and there are certain minimum requirements which are needed to maintain efficiency.

Records will depend largely on the craft involved, and the extent of work which the craft are engaged on. Also, as the general foreman is responsible for men and materials as well as work carried out, a certain amount of his administration requirements can be designated to the craft foremen.

RECORDS FOR ANY CONTRACT

These may be grouped under four main headings: Labour, Materials, Plant, and Progress.

Labour Other than time sheets [previously covered], a Time Book or Labour Allocation Book may be used to record all forms of labour and would include: (i) daily record of 'ordinary time' hours worked, plus overtime hours; (ii) weekly bonus payments, or incentives involved; (iii) any guaranteed time in the event of loss by weather; (iv) expenses involving travelling and subsistence etc; and (v) daywork (in hours) covering all variations.

Materials The ordering and requisition of materials has already been dealt with including stock checks. A Materials

Received Book, should be kept in which any appropriate advice notes or delivery notes can be filed or noted. The Invoice, which gives the same information as the delivery note may be forwarded to the foreman for checking, but should afterwards be returned to head office.

Plant A Plant Record Book, or Weekly Plant Record Sheet, should be prepared in duplicate, one copy held on site and the other sent to head office, and this should include the following information: (i) the firm's plant requisitioned for site use; (ii) any plant which is on hire; (iii) the weekly return should give daily working or standing time for each machine; (iv) details of non-mechanical plant or power tools; and transfer or movement of plant with dates.

The above information collected during a contract would enable an accurate assessment to be made by costing clerks on the usage, should this be necessary to be entered as a charge on the contract.

Progress An Acknowledgement Book is useful to confirm the receipt of any instructions from the architect, clerk of works, or general foreman etc. This should be used in triplicate, one copy should be given to the person giving the instructions, one copy to head office, and the third retained by the foreman on the site. Progress recorded by a general foreman would normally be done in a Contract Progress Report, a weekly report which would be filled in daily.

Progress and the craft foreman The trade and size of the job may not demand any records being kept by the craft foreman as outlined under the previous four headings. It may be the firm's policy that the general foreman shall maintain and keep the site records, particularly those dealing with labour, materials, and plant, especially on large jobs. In his own interests, the craft foreman should keep a daily record or diary, and this may include much of the relative information suggested in the preceeding four headings.

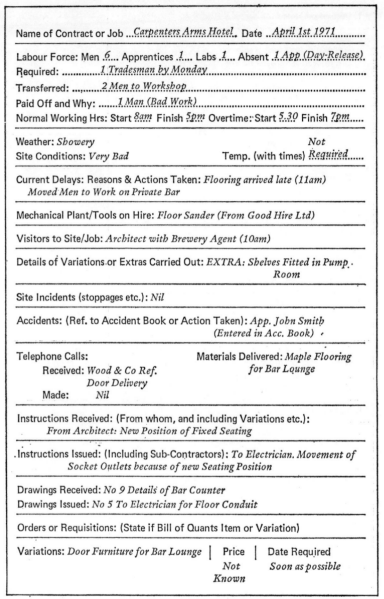

Name of Contract or Job ...*Carpenters Arms Hotel*. Date ..*April 1st 1971*...........

Labour Force: Men .*6*... Apprentices .*1*... Labs .*1*... Absent .*1 App. (Day-Release)*.
Required: ....*1 Tradesman by Monday*...
Transferred: ..,.......*2 Men to Workshop*...
Paid Off and Why: ......*1 Man (Bad Work)*...
Normal Working Hrs: Start *8am* Finish *5pm* Overtime: Start *5.30* Finish *7pm*......

Weather: *Showery*   *Not*
Site Conditions: *Very Bad*   Temp. (with times) *Required*......

Current Delays: Reasons & Actions Taken: *Flooring arrived late (11am)*
  Moved Men to Work on Private Bar

Mechanical Plant/Tools on Hire: *Floor Sander (From Good Hire Ltd)*

Visitors to Site/Job: *Architect with Brewery Agent (10am)*

Details of Variations or Extras Carried Out: *EXTRA: Shelves Fitted in Pump .*
                                            Room

Site Incidents (stoppages etc.): *Nil*

Accidents: (Ref. to Accident Book or Action Taken): *App. John Smith*
                                        (Entered in Acc. Book) ·

Telephone Calls: Materials Delivered: *Maple Flooring*
    Received: *Wood & Co Ref.*   *for Bar Lounge*
              Door Delivery
    Made: *Nil*

Instructions Received: (From whom, and including Variations etc.):
    From Architect: New Position of Fixed Seating

.Instructions Issued: (Including Sub-Contractors): *To Electrician. Movement of*
    Socket Outlets because of new Seating Position

Drawings Received: *No 9 Details of Bar Counter*
Drawings Issued: *No 5 To Electrician for Floor Conduit*

Orders or Requisitions: (State if Bill of Quants Item or Variation)

Variations: *Door Furniture for Bar Lounge* | Price | Date Required
                                    Not   *Soon as possible*
                                    Known

Fig 68   The craft foreman's daily diary

1. Injured persons Full Name & Address:	Age:
2. Date & Time of Accident: Where did Accident Happen?: Did injured employee notify Accident?: Date & Time he left work:	
3. Occupation in which employed: Was he so engaged when Accident Happened?: How long has he been in your employment?:	
4. Is injured person married?: If so, state No. of dependants:	
5. If single, has injured person any dependants?: If so, who?:	
6. Total wages paid for 12 months prior to Accident: Total wages paid (if employed under 12 months): Will he be paid wages during incapability?:	
7. Cause of Accident, give full details:	
8. Name of Person in Charge:	
9. Nature of injury: Regions injured or part of body: Right side or left side:	
10. Through who's neglegence did Accident happen?: Was injured person sober at time of Accident?: Was he guilty of misconduct or disobedience?: If so, give full details:	
11. Names of persons present or witnesses:	
12. If taken to Hospital, state name: Admittance as "In" or "Out-patient": If otherwise, name and address of Medical Attendant:	
13. Was First Aid given, if so — by whom: Nature of First Aid given:	
14. If still in Hospital, or when discharged?:	
15. Whether returned to work, if so — when?:	
16. Any other relevant details:	

A Medical Certificate, (if issued), should be furnished with these particulars.

Signed By: ....   Position with Firm: ....

Date: ....

Fig 69   An accident report form

THE FOREMAN'S DAILY DIARY

This should be compiled in a systematic manner, if a proper printed form is not available. The information recorded should be concise, yet sufficient to clarify any future problem which may arise. There are diaries published, which are admirable for supervisory staff, and the type of daily entries would be as follows:

1. *Accidents*: (i) the firm if employing 20 men or more should have a safety officer, who would be responsible for for the reporting of accidents; (ii) because of various sites, the safety officer may employ a system of reporting accidents to him by accident report form; (iii) on large jobs or firms, where there is a person trained in first aid, his assistance should be sought in compiling the accident report; and (vi) if the craft foreman [being the only one on a site or acting general foreman] is responsible for accident reporting, he should acquaint himself with:
   Form No 43B, 'Notice of Accident or Dangerous Occurence'.
   Book BI 50, 'Accident Book' (National Insurance Act).
   Form SHW 6, deals with accidents resulting from contact with, or approach to, overhead lines on construction sites.

2. *Weather and site conditions*: (i) a full report would be an advantage later if bad work was criticised, such as action of early frost etc; (ii) a record of loss of working time, delays, or hold-ups due to site conditions; and (iii) the daily diary reports or records of continuous delays due to inclement weather or long periods of frost, or flooding, may be accepted as Acts of God, should the continuous delays extend the contract beyond a completion date.

3. *Incidents*: (i) any form of incident on site such as strikes, hold-ups, disturbances etc, may be reported under this heading; (ii) delays in receipt of instructions or drawings,

or changes in the contract or use of materials would be recorded; and (iii) other incidents may be accidents, power failures etc.

4. *Variations*: (i) record any instructions or references to orders received concerning variations; (ii) record dates when variation work started and was completed.

The above information on exact dates is vital where monthly payments are made or Interim Certificates issued [to be dealt with later].

5. *General Progress on Site*: (i) diary entries on site progress should be mainly devoted to items such as would be difficult to record on the progress chart previously dealt with; (ii) a daily entry helps in the compiling of a weekly report of the general work or stages done; (iii) where evidence of materials used, may be questioned at a later date—records of samples taken during the actual work may be useful later, eg weight of lead, or thickness of wood blocks etc, and (iv) photography is useful to record the progress of any site especially if several views are taken, and the dates of taking recorded on the prints.

Photographs could also be used to prove that certain actions were taken or types of construction employed, eg support of RC beams in curing, sealing of cavities or covered-up DPC's etc.

WORKMEN'S COMPENSATION

Information has already been given on the recording of accidents in the accident book, and the filling in of an accident report. In some instances, accidents which are caused by negligence on the part of the employer resulting in severe injury, may lead to the operative later claiming Workmen's Compensation.

The following notes will give guidance in situations where the nature of injury or evidence of negligence would suggest that a compensation claim is likely:

The accident should be entered in the accident book.

If the accident is severe, the local factory inspector should be informed immediately or within 3 days. The foreman should acquaint himself with the address of the nearest factory inspector.

If the injured worker's insurance card is held on site, this should be forwarded to the firm's office.

Get the firm to notify their insurance company of the accident, giving as many details as possible.

If the accident or injury was due to wilful negligence on anyone's part, try and get the names and addresses of any witnesses [this includes the public] and if possible obtain from them a signed statement.

If the injured worker has failed to report the accident at once [and it is not apparent] an explanation should be demanded and given in any report.

If there is suspicion of an operative malingering, or any injury being due or connected with any previous accident or employment, particulars of previous employers may be useful in building up the facts.

It may be that the firm, or the foreman acting on the firm's behalf, may deny liability of any compensation claim, but this should not be stressed unless instructions to this effect have been given by the insurance company.

M

PART FOUR

MEASUREMENT

25

Calculations of Quantities

Before any form of building work is started, some form of estimate must be provided by the contractor, perhaps against competition, to ascertain what the job will necessitate in terms of materials to do the job, labour to perform the task, and the profit margin covering the firm's overheads and expenses in order to keep the firm in business.

Where the job is small, an estimate can be made from experience in the trade, or of similar work, but for large contracts the question of labour and materials must be accurately assessed, otherwise the firm's 'Tender' or estimate for the job will not get very far against strong competition.

Labour and materials To analyse the items of work and materials needed from a drawing and specification, which in themselves do not give this information, the drawing is studied and the required information extracted after comparing the item with its relevant form of measurement contained in 'The Standard Method of Measurement'. The Standard Method of Measurement, or SMM, covers all the building trades, and its use in the extraction of items of work and materials leads to the compiling of, 'The Bill of Quantities'.

Purpose of the Bill of Quantities is to enable several contractors to tender for work on the same basis. The Bill breaks down the operation into parts and trades, thus enabling certain sections to be open for sub-contracting. The bill describes the quantity and quality of the work. It provides a basis for ordering materials and financial control and costing of the job. The bill does not override any conditions or agreements which are related to the contract.

The Specification is a detailed written statement describing the standard or finish of work, where or in what manner items should be fixed, the dimensions or quality etc. Where a bill of quantities exists, a specification would be rare, as it is not regarded as a contract document; and where a specification exists with a bill it would merely fill the gap between the drawings and the bill. If a specification is used or not, it is important to note that no contractural argument can be settled by reference to the specification. Where specifications are not issued with bills of quantity, Preamble Clauses are introduced to specify material and workmanship standards.

Quantities and Price By agreement between the NFBTE and the Royal Institute of Chartered Surveyors, quantities are deemed not to be required for work valued up to £8,000, but required in excess of £8,000, but this agreement has no lawful backing. For jobs over £8,000, the standard RIBA form of contract with a bill of quantities is nearly always used.

Preparing the Bill As previously stated, the methods of measuring the various items of work are laid down in the SMM. Preparing the Bill consists of four main operations: Taking Off, Squaring, Abstracting, and Billing.

Taking Off According to the methods of measuring laid down in the SMM, the items from the drawings are recorded on Taking Off, or Dimension Paper. Some items are measured by length [lineal]; some length by breadth [superficial]; some by three dimensions [cubical]; while some are referred as items because they are jobs or operations which would be difficult to measure.

The recording of the items on the dimension or taking off paper, is done under columns, and reference should be made to the example given at the end of this Chapter.

1st column—is used mainly for reference numbers to the items.

2nd column—this column is known as the 'Timesing' column, where the number of times that a particular item or dimension is measured is recorded.

3rd column—the actual dimensions.

4th column—the result of columns 2 and 3 or 'Squaring'.

5th column—a description of the item of work usually recorded in abbreviated form [see the list of abbreviations].

Squaring is the mathematical multiplication of columns 2 and 3, and recorded under column 4.

Abstracting is the sorting out of all the items which have been 'taken off', measured, and described on the taking off sheets, and arranged as totals under the various trades.

Billing is the last operation in making the bill of quantities, and consists of the abstracted items being compiled in a book-like list of labour and materials with costs.

The Billing Paper is divided into six columns as follows:

1st column—the reference or item.

2nd column—description of the item.

3rd column—quantity of the previous item.

4th column—the unit of measure of the quantity.

5th column—the rate or unit price.

6th column—the cost or amount in pounds.

ABBREVIATIONS USED IN QUANTITIES

a.b.	As before	F.C.	Fair cutting.
a.b.d.	As before described	fcd.	Faced.
ard.	Around	fcgs.	Facings.
asp.	Asphalt	flg.	Flooring.
av.	Average	fwk.	Formwork.
av.d.	Average depth	frd.	Framed.
bd'g.	Boarding	frm.	Frame.
B. & P.	Bed and point	G.I.	Galvanised iron.
b.e.	Both edges	Grd.	Ground.
	Bossed ends	g. & v.	Grain and varnish.
Bk.	Brick	H.B.	Half brick.
b.m.	Birdsmouth	H.B.S.	Herringbone strutting.

b.n.	Bullnosed	H.R.	Half-round.
B. on E.	Brick on edge	hd.c.	Hardcore.
B.p.p.	British polished plate	ht.	Height.
bldg.	Building	h.w.	Hardwood, hollow wall.
b/s	Both sides	I.C.	Inspection chamber.
B.S.B.	British Standard Beam	inc.	Include.
bwk.	Brickwork	intl.	Internal.
C.A.	Cart away	j'nt.	Joint.
C.B.	Common brick	j'st.	Joist.
C. & P.	Cut and pin	K.S. & P.	Knot, stop, and prime.
chf'd.	Chamfered	lab.	Labour.
chy.	Chimney	l & m.	Labour and materials.
C.I.	Cast iron	lin.	Lineal.
Cir.	Circular	l & p.	Lath and plaster.
C.L.M.	Cement-lime mortar	l.c. & w.	Labour cutting and waste.
C.M.	Cement mortar		
Co.	Course	l.p.f. & s.	Lath, plaster, float and set.
C.P.	Chromium-plated		
ct.	Cement	L.M.	Lime mortar.
c. & w.	Cutting and waste	l.r. & s.	Lath, render and set.
csk.	Countersunk	meas'd.	Measured.
cub.	Cube or cubic	m.c.	Metal casement.
cupd.	Cupboard	M.H.	Man-hole.
ddt.	Deduct	mk'g gd.	Making good.
D.C.S.F.	Deal cased sash frame	M.L.	Milled lead.
D.H.	Double hung	mis.	Mitres.
Diam.	Diameter	msd.	Measured.
Dist.	Distemper	m/s	Measured separately.
D.P.C.	Damp proof course	m. o/s	Measured one side.
ea.	Each	n.e.	Not exceeding.
E.O.	Extra over	n.w.	Narrow widths.
e.g.	Eaves gutter	o/s.	One side.
e.s.	Edges shot	p. & c.	Parge and core.
exc.s.t.	Excavate surface trench	p.f.	Plain face.
etl.	External	P. & S.	Planking and strutting.
f.a.i.	Fresh air inlet	P.C.	Prime cost.
founds.	Foundations	P. ct.	Portland cement.
f.f.	Fair face	P.C.C.	Portland cement concrete.
Pl. Bd.	Plaster board	T. & G.	Tongue and grooved.
Prov. S.	Provisional sum	t. & r.	Treads and risers.
R. & S.	Render and set	V.	Varnish.
r. & g.	Rubbed and gauged	V.P.	Vent pipe.
reb'd.	Rebated	W.	Wrot
r.c. & w.	Raking, cutting and waste	W. & frd.	Wrot and framed
r.c.	Reinforced concrete rough cut	wd'w.	Window.
		W.I.	Wrought iron.
R.F. & R.	Return, fill, and ram	W. o/s.	Wrot. one side
r.f. & s.	Render, float, and set	W'thd.	Weathered.
r.o.j.	Rake out joints	w.s. & 3	Wash, stop, and three oils.
r.o. & p.	Rake out and point		

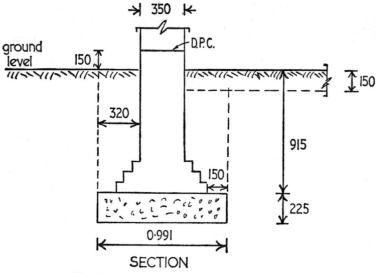

Fig 70   A section of the quantities example

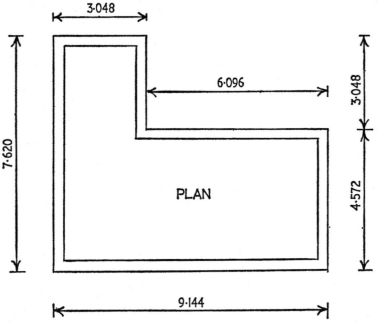

Fig 71   A plan of the quantities example

R.S.J.	Rolled Steel Joist	wt.	Weight.
retd.	Returned	Yd.	Yard.
ro.	Rough	Y.s.	York stone.
R.W.P.	Rain water pipe	x grain	Cross grain.
S.P.	Soil pipe	x tgd.	Cross-tongued
sk.	Sunk	xtg.	Existing.
Sk.b.	Skew-back	2ce.	Twice.
Sq.	Square	3ce.	Three times
s.w.	Stonewear		
S.T.	Surface trench		
sup.	Superficial		

The Calculation of quantities As the foreman will become acquainted with the bill of quantities and the materials and labour items connected with his trade, it is essential that he should have some idea as to how the bill has been compiled, and an interpretation of how the abbreviations are applied. It is hoped that the following example, although of an elementary and general type, will at least help to show the process of taking off, abstracting, and billing the items.

Example: Prepare the Taking Off, Abstracting, and Billing of the Quantities required for the building shown in part in Figs 70 and 71, and the following specification: (i) sod and soil stripping 150mm deep over the area, and being deposited on site after wheeling an average of 10m; (ii) excavations of trenches to provide for wall foundation and footings; (iii) the return, filling, and ramming of excavated earth around the foundations; (iv) load and cart away the surplus earth from the above excavation to a tip, and (v) provide for the planking and strutting for the above excavation.

Taking Off: Alongside the 'Taking Off' dimensions, notes and references are given from the 'Standard Method of Measurement',—5th Edition, Metric.

Abstracting: It will be noted that the items measured in metres are transferred to the 'Bill' to the nearest whole metre, eg 3.400 equals 3 square metres, while 3.500 equals 4 square metres.

Wall Thickness: In the example the wall thickness is booked as 1½ bricks, and for dimension purposes comprises 1 brick (225mm), plus ½ brick (112.5mm), plus a mortar joint of 12mm, which equals—say 350mm.

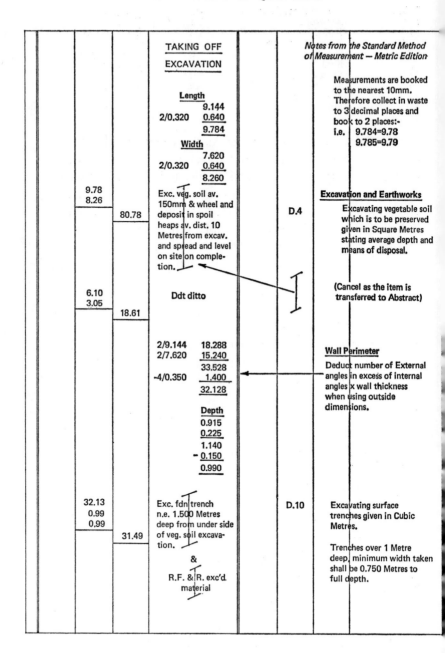

			TAKING OFF			Notes from the Standard Method of Measurement — Metric Edition
			EXCAVATION			Measurements are booked to the nearest 10mm. Therefore collect in waste to 3 decimal places and book to 2 places:- i.e. 9.784=9.78 9.785=9.79
			Length 9.144 2/0.320 0.640 9.784 **Width** 7.620 2/0.320 0.640 8.260			
9.78 8.26	80.78		Exc. veg. soil av. 150mm & wheel and deposit in spoil heaps av. dist. 10 Metres from excav. and spread and level on site on completion.		D.4	**Excavation and Earthworks** Excavating vegetable soil which is to be preserved given in Square Metres stating average depth and means of disposal.
6.10 3.05	18.61		Ddt ditto			(Cancel as the item is transferred to Abstract)
			2/9.144 18.288 2/7.620 15.240 33.528 -4/0.350 1.400 32.128 **Depth** 0.915 0.225 1.140 - 0.150 0.990			**Wall Perimeter** Deduct number of External angles in excess of internal angles x wall thickness when using outside dimensions.
32.13 0.99 0.99	31.49		Exc. fdn trench n.e. 1.500 Metres deep from under side of veg. soil excavation. & R.F. & R. exc'd. material		D.10	Excavating surface trenches given in Cubic Metres. Trenches over 1 Metre deep, minimum width taken shall be 0.750 Metres to full depth.

	32.13 0.99 <u>.31.81</u>		Level and ram bottom of excvn to receive concrete.	D.17	(a) Treating surface of ground measured in Square Metres.
		4/2/0.4955	32.128 <u>3.964</u> 36.092		
	36.09 0.15 <u>5.41</u>		P & S to sides of open excv'n commencing at ground level n.e. 1.500 Metres dp.		
2/	32.13 .99 <u>63.62</u>		P & S to sides of s.t. excv'n commencing below vegetable soil & n.e. 1.500 Metres dp. (b.s.m.)	D.20	**Planking and Strutting** Taken to full depth of any excavation over 300mm deep. Given in Square Metres.
			(Alternatively an Average on the Centre Line can be taken):-		
			$+\dfrac{150}{2}$ 0.990 0.075· 1.065.		
2/	32.13 1.07		P & S to side of s.t. excv'n commencing 75mm below g.l. and n.e. 1.500 Metres deep.		
			CONCRETE WORK		**Concrete Work**
	32.13 0.99 0.23 <u>7.32</u>		1:2:4 Portland cmt. concrete in fdns. ex 150mm n.e. 300mm thick.	F.3	(a) Concrete in Foundations given in Cubic Metres in stages:-
			&		(i) Not exceeding 150mm thick.
			Ddt R.F. & R.		(ii) Ex. 150mm n.e. 300mm thick.
			&		(iii) Over 300mm thick.
			Add C.A. excv'd. material.		

Under D.17 description (diagram region): 0.4955, VEG. SOIL, 0.150, 0.990, ₵

			BRICKWORK UP TO D.P.C. LEVEL			Brickwork & Blockwork
			Height		G. (a)	Brickwork two Brick thickness and over reduced to one Brick (in Abstract and Bill), and given in Square Metres.
			0.915			
			0.150			
			1.065			
	32.13					Under two Bricks — thickness given in Square Metres stating the thickness.
	1.07		1½ B. wall in 2nd.			
		34.38	Hard Stocks in			
			c.m. (1:3) in			
			English Bond.		G.4	Brickwork in Projections reduced to one Brick thickness and given in Square Metres.
2/	32.13		½ B. in 2nd. Hard			
	0.23		Stocks in c.m. (1:3)			
		14.78	in projecting foot-			
			ings in Header Bond.			

FACINGS 75mm BELOW GROUND LEVEL

225mm

G.L.   D.P.C.

½B   1½B

CONCRETE FOUNDATION

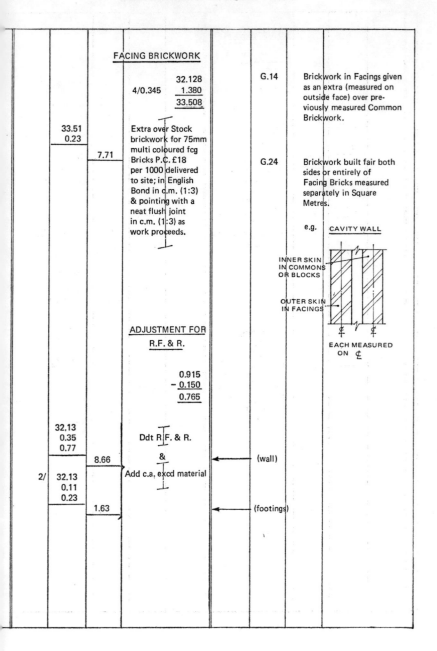

FACING BRICKWORK

			32.128 4/0.345 1.380 33.508	G.14	Brickwork in Facings given as an extra (measured on outside face) over previously measured Common Brickwork.
33.51 0.23		7.71	Extra over Stock brickwork for 75mm multi coloured fcg Bricks P.C. £18 per 1000 delivered to site; in English Bond in c.m. (1:3) & pointing with a neat flush joint in c.m. (1:3) as work proceeds.	G.24	Brickwork built fair both sides or entirely of Facing Bricks measured separately in Square Metres. e.g. CAVITY WALL

ADJUSTMENT FOR
R.F. & R.

			0.915 − 0.150 0.765

32.13 0.35 0.77	8.66	Ddt R.F. & R. & Add c.a, excd material	←	(wall)
2/ 32.13 0.11 0.23	1.63		←	(footings)

INNER SKIN IN COMMONS OR BLOCKS

OUTER SKIN IN FACINGS

EACH MEASURED ON ₵

			ADJUSTMENT FOR SURFACE STRIP AROUND PERIMETER		

ADJUSTMENT FOR SURFACE STRIP AROUND PERIMETER

```
                    36.092
        -4/0.320     0.640
                    35.452
35.45
0.32        Ddt c/a.
0.15
      1.70    &
           Add R.F. & R.
           excd material.
```

Adjustment of Surface Soil outside Building. previously measured as cart away. Therefore veg. soil deposited in spoil heaps will be on completion spread and levelled over site.

```
ITEM    Allow for keeping        D.19 (b)
        excavations free
        from general water.
```

Note:- 'Protection' items will also be taken to cover all Concrete and Brickwork.

	Items
G.70	Brickwork
F.68	Concrete

```
            D.P.C.
32.13
0.35    Horizontal D.P.C.
        of two courses of
  11.25  best Welsh slates
        laid breaking joint    G.44
        & bd'd & ptd in
        c.m. (1:3).
```

D.P.C.

D.P.C. over 225mm wide measured in Square Metres. Those 225mm wide and under measured in Lineal Metres stating width in description.

ABSTRACTING

EXCAVATIONS AND EARTHWORKS

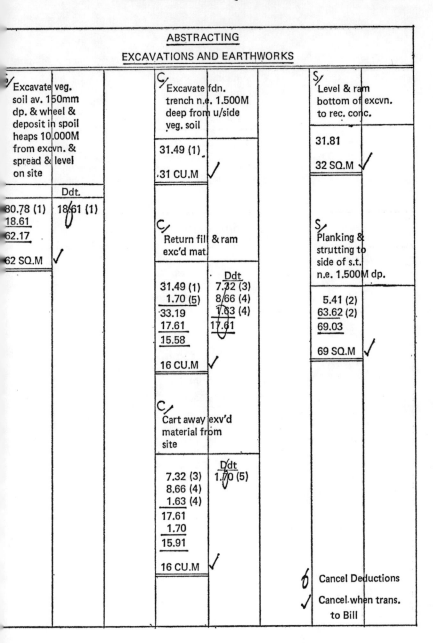

C/
Excavate veg.
soil av. 150mm
dp. & wheel &
deposit in spoil
heaps 10.000M
from excvn. &
spread & level
on site

	Ddt.
80.78 (1)	18.61 (1)
18.61	
62.17	
62 SQ.M ✓	

C/
Excavate fdn.
trench n.e. 1.500M
deep from u/side
veg. soil

31.49 (1)
.31 CU.M ✓

C/
Return fill & ram
exc'd mat.

	Ddt
31.49 (1)	7.32 (3)
1.70 (5)	8.66 (4)
33.19	1.63 (4)
17.61	17.61
15.58	
16 CU.M ✓	

C/
Cart away exv'd
material from
site

	Ddt
7.32 (3)	1.70 (5)
8.66 (4)	
1.63 (4)	
17.61	
1.70	
15.91	
16 CU.M ✓	

S/
Level & ram
bottom of excvn.
to rec. conc.

31.81
32 SQ.M ✓

S/
Planking &
strutting to
side of s.t.
n.e. 1.500M dp.

5.41 (2)
63.62 (2)
69.03

69 SQ.M ✓

ð   Cancel Deductions

✓   Cancel when trans.
    to Bill

CONCRETE WORK

C, 1:2:4 Portland
cement concrete in
fdn. ex. 150mm
n.e. 300mm thick

7.32 (3)

7 CU.M

BRICKWORK AND BLOCKWORK

S, 1½ Brick in 2nd.
Hard Stocks in
c.m. (1:3) in
English Bond

34.38 (3)

34 SQ.M

S, E.O. Stock Brick-
work for 75mm
multi-coloured
fcgs. P.C. £18 per
1,000 delivered
to site in
English Bond in
c.m. 1:3 and
pointing with a
neat flush joint
in c.m. 1:3

7.71 (4)

·8 SQ.M

S, ½ Brick in 2nd.
Hard Stocks in
c.m. (1:3) in
projecting foots.
in Header Bond

14.78 (3)

7.39 reduced to
1 Brick
7 SQ.M

S, Hor. D.C.P. two
courses of best
Welsh slates laid
breaking joint and
bed'd & pt'd in
c.m. (1:3)

11.25 (5)

11 SQ.M

Item No.	Description	Qty	Unit	Rate	£
	BILL No. 2				
	EXCAVATION AND EARTHWORKS				
	Preamble Clauses covering nature of ground, water level etc.	M			
	Excavate vegetable soil average 150mm deep and deposit in spoil heaps average 10 metres from excavation and spread and level over site on completion.	62	SQ		
	Excavate foundation trench not exceeding 1.500 metres deep from underside of vegetable soil excavation.	31	CU		
	Return fill and ram excavated material around foundation.	16	CU		
	Cart away excavated material from site.	16	CU		
	Level and ram bottom of excavation to receive concrete.	32	SQ		
	Planking and strutting to sides of trenches not exceeding 1.500m total depth from ground level.	69	SQ		
	Allow for keeping excavation free from general water.	ITEM			
	BILL No. 3				
	CONCRETE WORK				
	Preamble Clauses covering Materials, Mixes, Tests etc	M			
	1:2:4 Portland Cement concrete in foundations exceeding 150mm not exceeding 300mm thick.	7	CU		

N

Item No.	Description	Qty	Unit	Rate	£
	BILL No. 4				
	BRICKWORK AND BLOCKWORK				
	Preamble Clauses covering materials etc.				
	1½ Brickwork in 2nd Hard Stocks in English Bond in cement mortar (1:3)	M 34	SQ		
	1 Brick in 2nd. Hard Stocks in Header Bond in cement mortar in projecting footings.	7	SQ		
	Extra over 2nd Hard Stocks in English Bond for 75mm multi-coloured facings P.C. £18 per 1,000 delivered to site and add for profit; in English Bond in cement mortar (1:3) and pointing with a neat flush joint as work proceeds.	8	SQ		
	Horizontal D.P.C. of two courses of best Welsh sltates laid breaking joint and bedded and pointed in cement mortar 1:3	11	SQ		

26

Completed Work

MEASUREMENT OF BUILDING WORK

All building work is measured according to the principles laid down in the Standard Method of Measurement of Building Works. The standard method, was authorised by agreement between the Royal Institution of Chartered Surveyors and the National Federation of Building Trade Employers.

Measurement of completed work at stages for bonus or incentives Only work related to trades involved in bonuses or incentives need be measured. The bonus clerk or surveyor is not closely bound to the SMM, and can devise schemes of his own which are suitable to the measurement of labour only. The work would previously have been broken down into tasks, and the method of measurement agreed upon (eg in some types of work, brickwork might be better measured in stages rather than linear, superficial, or cubical). Having decided upon a unit of measurement, great care must be taken with recording so that measurement is not made of the same work done twice.

A Progress Book might be compiled outlining the operations and the value of this completed stage of work, and if only part of the operation has been completed the percentage value earned is recorded. Where a bonus clerk or surveyor is responsible for measurement, he should tour the site and take measurements in the presence of the trade foreman, so that any queries can be answered. Where there are several gangs in the same trade, a separate progress book should be compiled for each gang.

Where work cannot be standardised because of variations, the work done for each week would have to be measured with great care because of possible error being made through double measurement. Variable items are likely to be associated with such jobs as foundations, trenches, drains and soak-aways etc. In recording work done, the use of colours on the plans or programme to show the targets reached would be an advantage for reference purposes.

A thorough record of a gang's previous work performance would help with future likely performances. With incentive schemes, there is always a possibility that work might be scamped or the quality of work fall, therefore the foreman must try and maintain good standards so that when measurements are made, it will be in the interests of all.

MEASUREMENT OF COMPLETED WORK FOR INTERIM CERTIFICATES

Interim Certificates are issued by the architect at the end of various stages of the contract, so that the builder may receive payment for work done during this period. If interim certificates were not issued or these payments made to the builder, then over long contracts most builders would go bankrupt due to paying out for wages and materials and having to wait for repayment until the completion of the job.

The periods, at the end of which an interim certificate is to be issued, are described and provided for as an appendix to the RIBA Form of Contract (Clause 24 a, and b). Periods covering the issue of interim certificates on large contracts where the work is of a repetitive nature, such as housing estates, the interim certificates might be issued when the houses reach various levels, such as DPC, 1st floor, roof covering etc.

Amounts due for work done, and the cost of materials supplied to the site, will (subject to agreement between client and contractor), normally have two types of deductions: (i) Proportional Preliminaries costs; and (ii) Retention money.

Preliminaries costs may include such things as site clearance, trial holes, borings, or disposal of earth etc. If the preliminaries totalled £1,000 and the contract was due to last 10 months with monthly certificates, then £100 would be claimed on each certificate.

Retention Money the RIBA Form of Contract (Clause 24 c), states the percentage of 'Certified Value', to be retained by the client, and which is not to exceed 10 per cent. Also the clause states the limit of the Retention fund should not normally exceed 5 per cent of the contract sum, and it should be released in accordance with Clause 24 d (Name and Branch of Bank).

Measurement for Interim Certificates will include all the value of work done to date under the various trade headings, and including preliminaries and provisional sums, along with the value of unused or fixed materials on site. The value of the certificate will be the amount above, from which is deducted the amount of previous interim certificates plus 10 per cent retention.

Provisional Sum is a fixed amount included in a bill of quantities for a particular job of work to be executed within the limits of this figure, such as service connections, unloading or carriage that may entail cranes etc, or special installations, which are difficult to price exactly.

Prime Cost or (PC) Sum is a fixed amount included in a bill of quantities, for a fitting or component, such as a fireplace, door furniture, or sanitary goods to be supplied by a nominated supplier. This PC sum does not include labour or fitting costs, and would exclude any discount which the contractor may get from the nominated supplier.

VARIATIONS OR CONTRACT DEVIATIONS

Payment for building work is made by the client to the builder on the basis of an agreed contract price. Where there is no agreement, the employing client would be expected to pay a reasonable sum for the work carried out, and within an estimated price. Where additional work to that stated in the specification or contract is done, there must be some agreement made between the builder and the client or the architect acting on the client's behalf. Where additions or changes are made from the original work, these additions are called 'Variations'. Variations must be requested in writing on a Variation Order, and most contracts would provide and allow for variations to be made.

Variation Orders Clause 9, of the RIBA Form of Contract, contains provision by which the method is stated for any variations to be valid if an adjustment is to be made to the contract price. Although provision to order Variations is made in the RIBA Form of Contract, the extent to which they can be made is very wide. As a general rule, the contractor cannot be expected to carry out a variation if such work or change alters the entire scope or character of the contract. The variation order is issued to the builder by the architect, and should contain concise instructions [see example page 158].

Variations and Costs The RIBA form clause, provides that while additional work is to be valued in such a way as to permit a profit being made on the work done, there is no provision allowing the builder to recover any loss of profit for omissions of work.

Clause 11 (4), provides that if any omission should substantially change the conditions under which any remaining items of work are carried out, then this remaining work may be revalued at a reasonable rate.

Clause 11 (6), provides that where variation orders are made at the right time in relation to the work that is to be done, but where the timing may cause changes in the sequence of other site work, then the builder may recover costs covering the disruption for which there would be loss or expense and for which he could not recover payment by carrying out the additional work of a Variation Order.

Types of Variation Apart from variation orders given by the architect, variations may come about as a result of: (i) Provisional Bills, where there is likely to be site differences to the Bill of Quantities (eg depth of excavation or filling etc); (ii) PC Sums, the amount of profit and the cost of fixing the item concerned; (iii) Provisional Items, similar to Provisional Bills, but dealing with one item such as 'access boards to roof space' etc; (iv) Provisional Sums, such as for sewer connections where a sum is allowed, but where variations may be valued either (a) at rates contained in bill of quantities as long as the work is of a similar character, (b) at agreed rates based upon the bill's rates, or (c) day-work rates; and (v) Fluctuation of price changes in the costs of materials, or wage increases (or decreases if any occur!).

Measuring for variations The work to be carried out in the contract will already have been measured in the bill of quantities, therefore only the new variation or extra work need be measured, and this should be done in accordance with the Standard Method of Measurement and applicable to the item of work or material. Measurements should be made often, and recorded at the completion of each phase, or where there is a change in trades or in the use of materials, eg excavation of trench, concrete bed, and laying of pipes etc.

For the pricing of the variation order, the new work done (measured on site), shall be added; the corresponding work that would normally have been done under the contract (measured from the bill of quantities), shall be deducted.

With regards to the above paragraph, the smaller amount of price subtracted from the greater amount—shall be the amount of variation (either deducted or added), to the cost of the contract.

PART FIVE

JOINT INDUSTRIAL RELATIONS

27

Employers' Associations and Trade Unions

EMPLOYERS' ASSOCIATIONS

The rise of the trade unions led to the banding together of the employers in order that there might be some collective voice about wages and working conditions, in opposition to the demands, of the unions. In the first half of the nineteenth century, some employers' associations existed in the London area, and by the second half of the century had extended to many of the industrial areas throughout the country. It was around 1870, that a national General Builders' Association was formed, and later led to the establishment of various regional federations. Currently, there are two main employers' associations, the National Federation of Building Trade Employers and the Federation of Master Builders.

The National Federation of Building Trade Employers is the largest voice of the building industry today. It covers England and Wales and has 10 regional federations and some 300 local associations. In Scotland, there is a separate federation affiliated to the NFBTE with the prefix, Scottish NFBTE. Membership is open to all builders including general, craft, and sub-contractors, engaged in all aspects of building work.

Objectives and Service of the NFBTE:
1. They advise the Government of the day on all building matters.
2. They are the only building employers' organisation represented on all Government committees concerned with building.
3. They negotiate wages and conditions through the National Joint Council for the Industry, and operate machinery for the settlement of disputes.
4. They keep a watch on new legislation affecting employers, and give a full information service to members, as well as an advisory service to assist firms on management problems.
5. They represent building trade employers on the National Consultative Committee of Architects, Quantity Surveyors and Builders, the Joint Contracts Tribunal, the Confederation of British Industry, and the International Federation of Building and Public Works.
6. They administer the National Joint Apprenticeship Scheme through the National Joint Apprenticeship Board, and are represented on the Board of Building Education.
7. Local associations elect representatives to the Regional Federations' Councils, which in turn elect the National Council.

The Federation of Master Builders was formed during World War II, and came into being during the period of war damage in London. From a small nucleus of London builders, organisation spread rapidly throughout the United Kingdom, and in 1967 it was said there were some 20,000 building firms in membership. The main emphasis of the Master Builders has always been to afford service to the medium size and smaller undertakings.

Policy and Constitution of the Federation:
1. To further the interests of the building industry through

the federation on a national basis, in order to establish unity, protection, and solidarity of purpose.

2. To preserve by mutual association with professional institutes and societies, the established ideals for the well being of the industry, to obtain equitable forms of contract. To collate and tabulate technical and general information and data on all matters of interest to the industry.

3. To seek representation on and co-operation with ministries and committees set up for the purpose of dealing with all legislation, research etc, concerning the industry.

4. To plan and maintain close co-operation with the NFBTO. To stimulate interest in and agreement upon educational facilities for apprentices and learners under 21 years of age. To explore every avenue with the object of improving the conditions of the whole industry in collaboration with the operatives.

5. To develop within the trade the consciousness of the national importance of the industry and to foster a spirit of close co-operation between master builders individually.

6. To advocate a democratic autonomy of the industry, the permanent registration by the industry of all master builders.

7. To take into consideration the qualifications and standing of all master builders and firms seeking admission.

8. To disseminate to members, information on all matters of interest to the industry.

9. To co-operate with federations and associations of all allied trades, merchants, manufacturers etc, connected with the industry.

10. To promote excellence in the construction of building and just and honourable practice in the conduct on business, and to suppress malpractice.

The National House Builders Registration Council At the time of composition, there were some 11,500 house-building firms in England, Wales, and Scotland, accounting for 95 per cent of private sector housing, who were registered with the

National House Builders Registration Council. As the majority of craft foremen engaged on housing are likely to come in contact with the NHBRC requirements, the following brief notes are given for his guidance,

The NHBRC is an independent non-profit making body made up of two-thirds non-builders and one-third builders. Among the members are representatives from the following: The Building Societies Association; The Royal Institute of British Architects; The Royal Institute of Chartered Surveyors; Building Employers' Organisations; Building Trade Unions; and The Consumer Council.

Government observers attend all meetings. At Government request, the NHBRC set up a register of housebuilders, and the council can remove from the register any builder who in its view is not fit to be included taking into account the builder's work as a whole, including his after-sales service.

There are two main NHRBC requirements that all registered housebuilders must carry out in connection with every house built for sale: every house must be built to the standard laid down in the Council's 'Technical Requirements for the Design and Construction of Dwellings', and they must enter into the council's legal agreement to provide the purchaser with the protection of a 10 year guarantee scheme.

The Ten Year Guarantee

1. When the NHBRC is satisfied that a house has been built to their requirements, a certificate is issued to the purchaser bringing the guarantee into operation.
2. Under the guarantee, for the first 2 years the owner of a house will have defects rectified by the builder [or the NHBRC in case of the builder's default].
3. For a further 8 years, the owner is protected against major structural defects (which do not not include normal shrinkage, or wear and tear).
3. The NHBRC also undertakes to honour any award made by an arbitrator, if for any reason the registered housebuilder should default in meeting an award.

RISE OF TRADE UNIONS

A trade union has been defined as, 'a group of people organised in a particular way to achieve a particular purpose'. The purpose may differ according to trade, or change from time to time. Trade unionists, as members of a union cannot achieve their objective unless they share common ideas and agree to operate within a generally accepted constitutional framework.

A trade union must have (i) a philosophy, or collection of ideas which are shared by all active members; and (ii) a structure, or collection of rules which regulate the relationship of one member to another and the way in which the group as a whole reach their decisions.

Object of the Trade Union Movement (according to the TUC): 'Include the maintenance and improvement of wages, working conditions, and living standards, the assurance to workpeople of adequate opportunities for suitable employment and the implementation of their right to share in the control of Industry'.

History of Trade Unionism:
Since the early part of the eighteenth century, workers in a variety of trades had combined or bonded together to maintain standards of living and working conditions. It is only possible within the contents of this publication to provide a brief outline of the main events that occurred in the TU history:

Act of 1799: Prohibited TUs with severe penalties, or the meeting together of workers to discuss working conditions.

Act of 1802: A Factory Reform Act, which improved the conditions of apprentices.

Acts of 1819 & 1831: Restricted the employment of children and young people in cotton mills.

Act of 1833: Prohibited the employment of children under the age of nine except in silk mills, and night work under the age of eighteen except in lace manufacture.

In 1839: Nine hours a day and forty-eight hours a week was advocated for children under the age of thirteen. Lord Ashley pressed for a ten hour day and enquiry into conditions of women and children employed in mines.

Act of 1842: Prohibited the employment of women and children below ground.

Act of 1844: Prohibited night work for women and a maximum of twelve hours a day.

After 1825: There followed a movement for the formation of large and powerful federations in cotton and building.

1834: An old system of supplementing farm labourers' wages from the poor rates was discussed in Parliament.

1836: Pottery manufacturers formed a combination to resist trade unionists.

In the 1830's: Robert Owen, a cotton spinner and one of the greatest of the social reformers, formed the Grand National Consolidated Trade Union, which had 500,000 members.

Tolpuddle Martyrs: In 1834, the deportation of six Dorset farm labourers to Australia caused public opinion to change the course of the penalty which was put on them. They had been found guilty of helping to form a local trade union branch.

1850: The Amalgamated Society of Engineers was founded.

1860-70: Amalgamated principles in the building trade was formed under the leadership of Robert Applegarth, a carpenter.

1870: The first International Trade Union Congress was held (Applegarth was a member of the Council).

Trade Union Act of 1871: Made funds of a trade union safe, but allowed for a union to be sued and to sue.

1875: The Conspiracy and Protection of Property Act, prevented the prosecution of trade unionists for doing anything which would not have been criminal if done by an individual.

TU Congress of 1874: There were 1,100,000 members, of

which 250,000 were miners, an equal number were cotton workers, and 100,000 farm labourers.

Trade unions and politics Until the mid-eighties, trade unions were untouched by Socialist theories. An onslaught on the role of TUs was made by John Burns and Tom Mann, who were influenced by the teachings of Karl Marx and Henry George. They called for lower rates of subscription to recruit the lower paid workers.

It was in the late eighties that the unions drew closer together and formed federations, the Miners' Federation of 1888, and the Engineers' & Shipbuilders' of 1889.

In 1899, the Trade Union Congress weaned from Liberal allegiance and instructed its parliamentary committee to summon a conference of Socialist Societies—the Independent Labour Party, the Social Democratic Federation, and the Fabian Society—to concert measures for increasing the number of Labour members in Parliament. In 1906, the Labour Representation Committee became the Labour Party.

Other Important Dates

1901: A railway company sued a trade union for damages due to strike action, and a verdict was given in favour of the company.

1910: Trade Union membership was 2,565,000 which rose some three years later to 4,135,000.

1911: Seamen and firemen struck successfully for higher wages.

1906: The Trades Dispute Act, recognised strike action as a means of bargaining.

1910–13: Between these dates, transport workers flocked into the unions. In 1913, there were 113,000 teachers and 235,000 public employees in the unions.

1913: The Trade Union Act, before engaging in political activities, a trade union must secure approval of the majority of its members by vote in a special ballot.

1926: The General Strike.

o

Trade Unions and Building Many of the building craft unions had their origin in trade clubs of the eighteenth century, while some can even provide their history in the form of gradual development from the medieval Guilds. Whatever the foreman or building employee may think about trade unions, or being a member of same, it may be worth reflecting that early in the 1800s the following was written in a builders' journal: 'A Union founded on right and just principles is all that is now required to put poverty and the fear of it for ever out of society'.

It is impossible within the scope of this publication to give an account of the history of the building trade unions, because of the various trades involved and their vast and progressive evolutions. Below is listed some of the more important dates of events, which may help to show how the building unions have progressed and that comparisons may be made with modern times.

Important Building Union Dates:

1799: This is the date to which some trade clubs of carpenters and joiners can be traced.

1825: Carpenters stopped work on Buckingham Palace declaring the job 'black', and attempts to bring out non-union men turned the issue into a fight which required the Coldstream Guards to subdue.

1827: The Friendly Society of Operative Carpenters and Joiners was formed.

1889: The National Society of Bricklayers was formed.

1832: The Great Operative Builders' Union was formed and although it had some 40,000 members in 1834, passed out of existence in December of that year after failing over a dispute.

1830's: Robert Owen was responsible for changing the views held by the building trade unions, by stressing the need for co-operation between employer and operative, and not a form of militance.

1853: An agitation for a nine hour working day was begun by the Masons.

1859: There was a dispute which had important results—the lock-out of building operatives in London following the claim for a nine hour day. It was a drawn battle ending with the withdrawal by the employers of 'the document', which had made its usual appearance, but without the unions gaining their objectives and 24,000 men were finally out of work.

1860: A linking of trade clubs into one organisation—the launching of the Amalgamated Society of Carpenters and Joiners, when contributions were 3d (1p) per week with an additional 3d (1p) for friendly benefits.

1861: The Associated Carpenters and Unions of Scotland was formally inaugurated.

It is worth noting that the above association compiled a list of towns showing working hours. Most worked Saturday afternoons and wages paid were:

Aberdeen: 57 hours, 18s (90p) to 19s (95p) per week.

Edinburgh: 57 hours, 22s (£1.10) per week.

Dumfries: 60 hours (21s) (£1.05) per week.

Glasgow: 57 hours, 5d (2p) per hour.

Dundee: 57 hours, 4d (1½p) per hour.

1877: A strike of joiners in Manchester lasted over a year.

1881: Of 95 Scottish Associated C. & J. Branches, 64 were working 51 hours per week, 6 were working 57 hours per week, and the remainder 54 hours, with wages varying from 5d (2p) to 7½d (3p) per hour.

1891: The Amalgamated Society of Carpenters and Joiners formally took over the 'Regular Carpenters' of the city of Dublin, who claimed direct descent from a medieval Guild of the fifteenth century.

1912: Arising from opinion expressed at the Trade Union Congress, the parliamentary committee arranged several conferences of building trade unions during the year, to frame a scheme for the amalgamation of all the unions engaged in the building industry.

1918: The National Federation of Building Trades Operatives was established [see later notes].

1923: An attempt was made unsuccessfully to amalgamate the

Amalgamated Society of Woodworkers and the Amalgamated Union of Building Trade Workers.

1926: The General Council of the TUC received a request from the AUBTW to call a conference of Building workers' unions towards the proposed project for one union for the building industry.

1927: The above requested conference was held, and was attended by representatives from all the building unions and the Engineering and Constructional Workers' Society, and although it was in favour of the principle of confederation, made no decision as the NFBTO had not committed itself to confederation and the AUBTW was seeking reaffiliation to the Federation.

1968: In December the Amalgamated Society of Painters and Decorators and the Amalgamated Society of Woodworkers signed a Statement of Intent setting out the principles of a merger.

It was also at this time, that the Amalgamated Society of Woodworkers announced that they had had discussions on the possibility of 'closer working or mergers' with the ABT, ASWM, AUBTW, and the NUFTC.

1970: On 1 January 1970 the Amalgamated Society of Painters and Decorators together with the Association of Building Technicians transferred their engagements to the Amalgamated Society of Woodworkers.

The National Federation of Building Trade Operatives The movement which resulted in the establishment of the NFBTO began in 1878, when the initiative was taken by the Operative Bricklayers' Society. They sent a circular inviting various unions in the building industry to send representatives to a meeting at their office on 27 February 1878, to discuss the advisability of adopting 'some practical form of effectual federation, calculated to help any Trade in the federation successfully through a struggle in which it may be involved when too great for its own resources'.

The above meeting led to a crowded conference later that year on 1 May, at which the following unions were present:

Amalgamated Society of Carpenters and Joiners; Amalgamated Society of Decorators and House Painters; Operative Bricklayers' Society; General Union of Carpenters and Joiners; Metropolitan Plasterers; National Association of Operative Plasterers; Operative Stone Masons' Society.

At the above conference, a resolution was carried 'That this meeting believes that it is desirable to form a National Federation of Building Trade Operatives, and pledges itself to use every means in its power to attain this desirable object'.

In 1880, rules were drafted with the title name of 'The National Unity of Building Trade Associations'. After submitting the draft rules to the unions in 1881, there was some opposition to the new unity for some years during which opinion was expressed for one union for the building industry.

Arising from the above opinion expressed at the TUC Congress, the Parliamentary Committee of that body arranged several conferences during 1912, to frame a scheme for the amalgamation of all the unions engaged in the building industry. The name of the proposed organisation was to be the Amalgamated Building Workers' Union, but in 1913 a new scheme provided for a new name, The Building Workers Union.

Within a year however, the country was plunged into World War I and it was during these war years that much valuable work was done by the National Associated Building Trades Council, which helped to convince building operatives of the importance of still closer unity. In 1917, a scheme was submitted to extend the Building Trades Council, which had no financial liability, into a real federation for mutual assistance.

Being approved by all the unions covering the building trades, the National Federation of Building Trade Operatives was formally established on 5 February 1918 at Manchester.

In July 1969, the NFBTO announced that its title was to become the National Federation of Construction Workers, and that the change would be a gradual one, 'corresponding to the merging, at present under way, of Unions in the Construction Industry'.

28

Negotiation and Conciliation

HISTORY, STRUCTURE AND PURPOSE

Any agreement or negotiations made on behalf of operatives in the building trade, whether it is for wages, conditions, rules, or conciliation, are made by the National Joint Council for the Building Industry (NJCBI).

The Council was formed in 1926, and consists at national, regional, area, and local levels of an equal number of representatives from employers and operatives. The National Joint Council makes the working rules for the industry, and meets every January to consider proposals for revision of their agreement, which may be made by either side the previous November. The Council deals with any disputes which may arise in the industry, and provision is made for the steps to be taken in the event of failure to agree.

History of the Joint Council
In 1899, the plastering trade made a national agreement under which local committees were set up to deal with trade disputes as they arose.

In 1904, a more elaborate scheme of conciliation was introduced covering bricklayers, masons, carpenters, joiners, which made provision for the setting up of local and area conciliation boards.

By 1914, a fairly comprehensive system of joint negotiation had been established, though in the main the agreements made were applicable mainly to local conditions.

In 1921, the National Wages and Conditions Council was formed, which had its origins in the various joint discussions in the Building Industry between 1918 and 1920, under the protection of a body called the Industrial Council for the Building Industry (Building Trades Parliament).

Between 1918 and 1920, wage rates in the industry were bad, and the area councils found the task of getting order so difficult, that they began to press for some national machinery. A national agreement of wages, working hours and conditions, was agreed in principle in 1920 by the national federations of employers and operatives, which led to the formation in 1921 of the National Wages and Conditions Council.

The above Council adopted a system of grading towns and localities for wages under their Grading Scheme, and on 1 June 1922 there were 13 different rates from 1s 8d (8½p) per hour Grade A, to 1s 3d (6p) for Grade D, with respective labourers' rates at 1s 3d (6p), and 11¼d (4½p) per hour.

In 1926, alterations were made to the national wages and conditions machinery to give more power to the Regional Joint Wages Committees to gain regional settlement. At the same time, the name of the council was changed to the National Joint Council for the Building Industry.

In September 1930, the trade unions affiliated to the Council gave notice of their intention to withdraw from the national agreement. Both sides appointed a negotiating committee to review the existing agreement, and form the basis for a new one. Joint negotiations were finalised in September 1931, and the new agreement which is the basis of the present machinery of negotiation in the building industry in England, Wales, and Scotland, came into operation on 14 January 1932.

From 1921 to 1930, Scotland was covered by the agreements of the NJC, but in 1930 withdrew and set up a separate Scottish NJC, which adopted a national agreement similar to that covering England and Wales. In April 1964, the Scottish Council was dissolved and the two councils and the separate agreements were merged in the National Joint Council.

Structure of the NJC:

Level	NFBTE Members	NFBTO Members
National	23	23
Regional	12	12
Area	5	5
Local	5	5

There are ten regional committees, which can appoint area committees at their discretion.

Purpose and duties of the NJC The main items which may be dealt with by the National Joint Council are those under Clause 4 of their 'Memorandum of Agreement', which are listed below with the number of the National Working Rule shown in brackets:

1. Rates of Wages, (National Working Rule 1).
2. Working Hours, (NWR 2); Conditions of Service and Termination of Employment, (NWR 2b).
3. Extra Payments, (NWR 3).
4. Overtime, (NWR 4).
5. Night Gangs, (NWR 5); Regular Night Work (NWR 5a).
6. Travelling and Lodgings, (NWR 6).
7. Guaranteed Payments in relation to Time Lost.
8. Termination of Employment.
9. Apprenticeship.
10. Holiday Payment, (NWR 4).
11. Safety, Health, and Welfare.
12. Recogniton of Union Representatives, (NWR 7).
13. Sub-contracting for Labour-only, (NWR 8).
14. Payment for Absence due to Sickness or Injury, (NWR 9).

Note: Wage rates are adjusted to take account of the average level of the Government's index of retail prices during the preceding twelve months, and although two million workers' wage rates are affected by the index, there are no two industries where the sliding scale works exactly in the same way.

The Working Rule Agreement Methods of dealing with any variation of the NJC working rules on a local basis, are laid down under the terms of, 'The Working Rule Agreement', contained under Rule 10, para (k), of the General Rules of the National Federation of Building Trade Operatives.

The Agreement reads as follow: 'The Federation Branch is the guardian of the Working Rule Agreement governing the rates of wages and hours and conditions of labour, and of any variation of the Agreement sanctioned by the NJC for the Building Industry applicable to its area. Any violation of the Working Rule Agreement must be immediately reported to the appropriate Local Employers' Association.

'A Local Joint Committee, representative of the operatives and employers in the area concerned should be appointed to deal with disputes arising in connection with the Working Rule Agreement. On failure to agree on the LJC, the disputed point or points should be reported without delay to the Regional Secretary. The attention of the Federation Branch is particularly drawn to the provisions of the Working Rule Agreement relating to overtime and to the issue of overtime permits.

'The policy of the Federation is to reduce the hours of labour and, as a consequence, to restrict overtime to the irreducible minimum.

'The Federation Branch has the authority to initiate variation amendments of the Working Rule Agreement, in accordance with the Rules and Regulations of the National Joint Council for the Building Industry, and all movements relating to the initiation of such proposed amendments must be reported to the Regional Secretary'.

Recognition of Trade Unon Officers Although the foreman

will be engaged in the enforcement of the National Working Rules, these rules and their content are more likely to be watched by trade union officials. As the foreman will come in close contact in such matters with trade union officers, some information is given below of the recognition of such officers under terms of National Working Rule 7, agreed by the NJC on 30 October 1968:

Full Time Trade Union Officers: (Para 1)

'A full-time officer of a trade union which is party to the NJC for the Building Industry shall, by arrangement with the employer's senior representative in charge and on presenting his credentials, be allowed access to a site, shop, or job in order to carry out his trade union duties and to see that the Working Rule Agreement is being properly observed'.

Federation Stewards: (Para 5)

'The NFBTO shall at its discretion appoint one of the recognised stewards as the Federation steward and issue credentials to him. The Federation steward shall normally be in the employment of the main contractor. The NFBTO Regional Secretary shall be responsible for notifying the employer, in writing, of the appointment of a Federation steward with a view to his recognition by the employer which recognition shall not unreasonably be withheld or withdrawn.

'Where for any reason whatsoever the employer declines or withdraws recognition of a Federation steward, notice shall immediately be given in writing to the NFBTO Regional Secretary; any subsequent difficulty shall be referred to the established joint industrial machinery,'

Federation Stewards' Duties: (Para 6)

The duties and functions of a Federation steward shall be:

'To represent the operatives on matters affecting more than one trade or union, and to consult with management thereon; to co-operate with management and to assist individual stewards in their negotiations; to act as the representative of the NFBTO Regional Secretary in ensuring that the Working Rule Agreement and the provisions of Rule 9 of

Constitution and Rules of the NJCBI relating to the handling of differences and disputes are properly observed.'

Management, Stewards and Work:
Para 11:   'Management shall give recognised union and/or
            Federation stewards reasonable facilities for
            exercising their proper duties and functions, and
            these facilities must not be unreasonably with-
            held and must not be abused.'
Para 12:   'No steward shall leave his place of work to con-
            duct union business without first notifying his im-
            mediate supervisor and obtaining permission, and
            then only to conduct such business as is urgent
            and relevant to the site, job, or shop.'
Para 13:   'A steward shall be subject to all the provisions of
            the Working Rule Agreement in the same way as
            any other workman; but no recognised steward
            shall be dismissed or otherwise penalised in any
            way whatsoever for carrying out his functions as
            a steward.'

29

Site Labour Difficulties

Most difficulties or disputes which arise on any building site, would no doubt come under the following headings: wages, bonus rates, working conditions, discipline, lack of welfare facilities, lack of equipment or plant, and the possible unjust assignment of work.

Handling complaints and site difficulties is one of the foreman's duties, and these should always be tackled while the problems are in their early stages. The foreman should inform the operatives of the recognised machinery and provision for the handling of complaints. If he has built up a good team spirit resulting in confidence and goodwill with the operatives, then he should be able to exercise mutual understanding with the men and quickly straighten out any difficulty. There should be provision and a recognised time when an operative can approach his foreman with any grievance or difficulty. If for some reason an operative wishes to have a fellow-worker with him for moral support in the airing of a grievance, the foreman should grant this privilege providing the situation does not become a 'gang-up'.

Grievances The following provision is made for site procedure in terms of grievances, under Para 10 of the National Working Rule No 7: 'An operative having an issue or grievance shall in the first instance raise it with his immediate supervisor and every effort should be made to reach a settlement at this level.

'Where the issue or grievance affect a group of operatives they must immediately refer the matter to their union steward who may proceed to take it up with the site or works manager, agent, or general foreman, or other person designated by management for that purpose.

'Where the issue or grievance affects the members of more than one Union, the Federation Steward shall deal with the matter in similar fashion.

'Where an issue or grievance cannot be resolved through the foregoing procedure it shall be the duty of the Union or Federation Steward to report the facts to the full-time Trade Union officer or to the NFBTO Regional Secretary, as the case may be.

'In the event that management and the full-time Trade Union officer or the NFBTO Regional Secretary are unable to resolve the difficulty it shall be the responsibility of both sides to progress the matter in accordance with the provisions and requirements of Rule 9 of the Constitution and Rules of the NJCBI.

'In the meantime there shall be no stoppage of work, restriction of hours worked, or reduction in output and the Stewards shall see that this requirement is carried out.

'In all instances it shall be the responsibility of both the Union and/or the Federation Steward and of management to communicate decisions to the operatives concerned.

'In the case of management having an issue or grievance the matter should immediately be referred to the Regional Joint Secretaries.'

Disputes Procedure Prior to 2 February 1970, any difference or dispute which may have arisen in any locality. or was likely to involve any party affiliated to the National Joint Council was dealt with in accordance with the procedure set out in 'The Agreement for the Prevention of Disputes in the Building Trade' [known as the 'Green Book Procedure or Agreement'] or the parallel 'Agreement for the Plumbing Trade'.

With effect from 2 February 1970, the responsibility for the settlement of all disputes and differences arising in the building industry was vested in the National Joint Council, and shall be dealt with in accordance with the revised Rule 9 of the Council's Rules [given below].

The principal requirements of Rule 9, are incorporated in the Working Rule Agreement as National Working Rule 10 [which is also given below]:

Rule 9, Disputes Procedure:

(a) A dispute or difference that involves or is likely to involve a member or members of any party affiliated to the Council shall be dealt with in the manner prescribed in this Rule. No strike, lockout, or other industrial action shall be taken by any party to a dispute before the procedure set out in this Rule has been exhausted.

(b) A dispute or difference which cannot be resolved within the Company (in the manner prescribed in National Working Rule 7) shall be reported to the appropriate local or regional officials (employer and operative) who shall confer immediately, and if it is necessary to do so, shall arrange for a reference to the joint machinery.

(c) Emergency procedure:
If direct action has been taken or threatened the local officials must immediately report to the Regional Joint Secretaries who shall take all practical steps to bring about a resumption of normal working. Failing settlement the Regional Joint Secretaries shall refer the dispute to the Regional Conciliation Panel which shall meet as soon as practicable and in any event within seven days. The findings of the panel shall be implemented by the parties at once.

(d) Normal procedure:
In all other cases the dispute or difference may be referred by the local officials to the Local Joint Committee which shall hear and determine it as soon as practicable and in any event within 21 days. The decision of the Local Joint Committee shall be final and binding unless notice of appeal is given by either of the parties to his Regional

Joint Secretary within seven days from the date of notification of the decision. There shall be a similar right of
appeal where the Local Joint Committee fails to reach
a decision.

(e) In London and Liverpool and in any area not covered
by a Local Joint Committee the reference shall be made
direct to the Regional Conciliation Panel.

(f) Appeals:
An appeal from the decision of a Local Joint Committee
or in the event of it failing to reach a decision shall be
heard and determined by the Regional Conciliation
Panel as soon as practicable and in any event within 21
days.

(g) The decision of the Regional Conciliation Panel shall be
final and binding (for the territory to which it applies)
unless notice of appeal is given by either party to the
Clerk of the National Joint Council within 21 days of the
date of notification thereof. A Regional Conciliation
Panel which fails to reach a decision may itself refer the
matter to the National Conciliation Panel, but in the
absence of such reference the parties concerned shall
have the right of appeal.

(h) Within seven days of an appeal being made the Regional
Joint Secretaries shall forward to the Clerk to the
National Joint Council the record of proceedings at the
Regional hearing.

(i) Subject to approval by the National Joint Secretaries
appeals from decisions of Regional Conciliation Panels,
or appeals in the event of their failing to reach agreement, shall be referred to the National Conciliation
Panel for hearing as soon as practicable. The decisions
of the National Conciliation Panel shall be final and
binding and its proceedings shall be reported to the
Council at its next meeting and be received and entered
upon the minutes.

(j) In the event of the National Conciliation Panel failing to
reach a decision in regard to any case it shall report

accordingly to the next meeting of the Council, whereupon it shall be the duty of the Council:

(i) To suggest a solution of the matter and refer it back to the National Conciliation Panel for the suggestion to be considered and a decision arrived at,

or

(ii) To decide whether to proceed to deal with the matter in accordance with the provision of Rule 13 hereof.

(k) The National Joint Secretaries shall have an overriding discretion after consulting the parties, to refer any dispute direct to the National Conciliation Panel.

(l) The procedure at hearings of Conciliation Panel cases shall conform to that laid down in the Regulations. Where interpretations of the National Joint Council's Agreement or elucidation of the Council's decisions appear advisable, advice or guidance may be sought through the Procedure Committee.

Working Rule 10—Disputes and differences arising between members of the bodies affiliated to the National Joint Council, or any of them, shall be dealt with, in the first instance, in the manner prescribed in Para 10 of National Working Rule 7, Site procedure—Grievances.

Where the parties, at site level, are unable to resolve the issue or grievance, they shall report accordingly to their respective local secretaries and the matter shall thereafter be progressed in accordance with the provisions of Rule 9 of the Constitution and Rules of the National Joint Council. It is a requirement of Rule 9 that no direct action be taken by any party to a dispute until the procedure laid down for the settlemen of disputes has been exhausted.

Union Stewards Mention has already been made of the full-time trade union officer and the federation steward. It is the union steward who, as the site representative, is the link between organised workers and their union, and the one union official who is likely to have the greatest contact [in disputes or otherwise] with the craft foreman.

In order that the foreman may be conversant with the official characteristics of the union steward, the following details under Para 2, 3, and 4, of the National Working Rule No 7, are given below:

Para 2: 'When an operative who has been in the employment of the employer for not less than one complete working week has been properly appointed a site, job, or shop steward in accordance with the rules of his Union, and has been issued with credentials, the Union shall notify the employer, in writing, of the appointment with a view to his recognition by the employer, which recognition shall not be unreasonably withheld or withdrawn.

'Where for any reason whatsoever, the employer withholds or withdraws recognition of an accredited steward, notice shall immediately be given in writing to the Union; any subsequent difficulty shall be referred to the established joint industrial machinery.'

Para 3: 'Management shall not be required to recognise for purposes or representation more than one officially accredited steward for each Trade or Union.

'Where, however, the nature of the job makes it necessary, and by prior agreement between management and full-time officer of the Trade Union concerned other stewards may be appointed to deal with purely Union Matters.'

Duties and Functions of the Union Steward: (Para 4)
'The duties and functions of the recognised steward shall be:

To represent the members of the Union or Trade employed on the site, job, or in the shop.

To use his best endeavours to ensure the proper observance of the Working Rule Agreement.

To consult where necessary with management thereon in accordance with the procedure in Para 10, and—

In the event of a failure to resolve a difficulty, to ensure that it is dealt with in accordance with the provisions of Rule 9 of the Constitution and Rules of the National Joint Council for the Building Industry.'

P

NATIONAL SCHEME FOR APPRENTICESHIP

The National Joint Apprenticeship Scheme was established by the National Joint Council for the Building Industry on 1 November 1945. In October 1966 the National Joint Apprenticeship Board (NJAB) became the National Joint Apprenticeship and Training Commission (NJATC). This apprenticeship scheme, re-named on 4 October 1971 the National Joint Scheme for Skilled Building Occupation, made provision for entrants joining industry at the age of 16, with further relaxation to enable entrants over the age of 18 to be trained in a building craft.

The scheme is based on the following principles:

1. Deed or Indenture: there are four parties in all deeds, viz the employer, the guardian, the apprentice, and a representative—being an employer of the appropriate Regional or Local Joint Apprenticeship Committee.
2. Period of Apprenticeship: the normal period (at present), shall be 4 years and shall not begin earlier than the apprentice's 16th birthday.
3. Period of Probation: this shall not exceed 6 months and shall be included in the period of Apprenticeship. The period of probation of a boy entering employment before his 16th birthday shall begin on that birthday.
4. Wages and Working Conditions shall be as laid down from time to time by the National Joint Council.
5. Wages During Absence from Work: An apprentice shall not be entitled to wages during absence from work (other than recognised holidays or attendance at Day Classes), except that during absence through sickness or injury caused by an accident, he shall be paid his wages during such absence but not for a longer aggregate period of 4 weeks in any one year and less benefits due to him under the National Insurance Acts, 1946, or any other Statutes, provided that his incapacity for work is certified by a doctor's certificate in request of period of absence.

6. Attendance at Technical Classes:

    (a) The employer shall pay wages in respect of attendance at classes during normal working hours and also fees charged for all classes.

    (b) The Technical Education of the apprentice shall start from the date of entry into employment.

    (c) Until the end of the School or College year in which he reaches the age of 18, the apprentice shall attend Technical Day Classes for 1 day, or 2 half-days, or an equivalent period of Block Release, and shall study for the Craft Certificate Examination in his Craft, or other approved Examination.

    (d) An apprentice who has obtained a Craft Certificate and who wishes and is recommended by the Principal of the Technical College to study for higher qualification, shall be allowed to continue to attend.

    (e) In addition to Day Classes, the apprentice must throughout the whole period of apprenticeship attend approved evening classes on such day or days as may be reasonably required by the Technical College.

    (f) Where the apprentice has obtained his Craft Certificate, and where the Principal of the Technical College recommends, and the Joint Apprenticeship Committee is satisfied that the apprentice is unlikely to benefit from further attendance—the Committee have the power to waive the obligation to attend.

    (g) The JAC may at its discretion, in a special case, at any time suspend the obligation on an apprentice to attend day and evening classes, where the Principal advises and the Committee is satisfied.

Regional Joint Apprenticeship Committees shall be set up in each region of the council, and shall consist of an equal number of employers and operatives not exceeding a total of ten, and other co-opted persons interested in building or juvenile employment as the board may from time to time approve provided always that the number of such co-opted persons shall not exceed one-quarter of the remainder of the committee.

No co-opted member shall be allowed to vote on any matter affecting an apprentice agreement, or advise on industrial conditions arising therefrom.

Local Joint Apprenticeship Committees shall be set up by the Regional Joint Apprenticeship Committee, and shall comprise an equal number of employers and operatives together with such other persons interested in building and general education as the Local Joint Committee may co-opt.

No co-opted member shall be entitled to vote on any matter.

Appendix 1

THE BUILDING REGULATIONS

'The Statutory Instruments, 1965 No 1373—Building and Buildings', is a publication more generally referred to as, 'The Building Regulations'.

The Regulations (made and laid before Parliament in 1965), came into operation on 1 February 1966, and are arranged into 15 main parts, as follows:

Part	Content
A	General.
B	Materials.
C	Resistance to Moisture.
D	Structural Stability.
E	Structural Fire Precautions.
F	Thermal Insulation.
G	Sound Insulation.
H	Stairways.
J	Refuse Disposal.
K	Open Space, Ventilation and Height of Rooms.
L	Chimneys, Flues, Hearths.
M	Heat Producing Appliances.
N	Drainage.
P	Sanitary Conveniences.
Q	Ashpits, Wells, Tanks and Cisterns.

The Regulations, contain a further 11 Schedules, the content of which are as follows:

Schedule   *Content*
1   Partially Exempted Buildings.
2   Giving of Notices and Deposit of Plans.
3   Forms of Application for Dispensation or Relaxation.
4   Areas where Special Treatment of Softwood Timber is Required.
5   Rules for the Calculation of Loading.
6   Rules for Determining the Dimensions of Certain Timber Members.
7   Rules for Satisfying Requirements as to Structural Stability of Certain Walls.
8   Notional Periods of Fire Resistance.
9   Rules for Calculation of Permitted Limits of Unprotected Areas.
10 Notional Designations of Roof Constructions.
11 Thermal Insulation.

Appendix 2

WARNING CAPTIONS FOR NFBTE SAFETY SIGNS

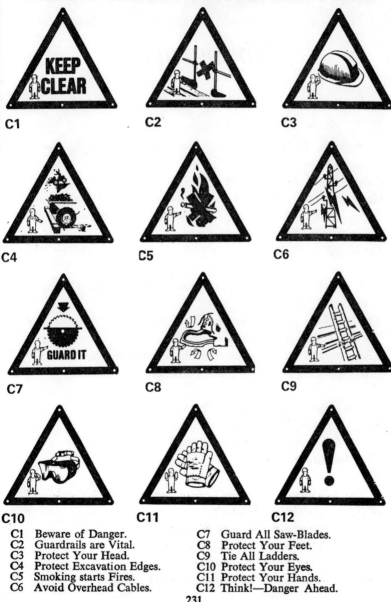

C1   Beware of Danger.
C2   Guardrails are Vital.
C3   Protect Your Head.
C4   Protect Excavation Edges.
C5   Smoking starts Fires.
C6   Avoid Overhead Cables.

C7   Guard All Saw-Blades.
C8   Protect Your Feet.
C9   Tie All Ladders.
C10   Protect Your Eyes.
C11   Protect Your Hands.
C12   Think!—Danger Ahead.

Bibliography

Broughton, H. F. *Economic Site Organisation & Building Supervision*

Calvert, R. E. *Introduction to Building Management*

Hollins, R. J. *Production and Planning Applied to Building*

Oxley, R. and Poskitt, J. *Management Techniques Applied to the Construction Industry*

Introduction to Foremanship published by the Institute of Industrial Administration

The Form of Contract published by the Royal Institute of British Architects

The Working Rule Agreement published by the National Joint Council for the Building Industry

The National Joint Apprenticeship Scheme and National Form of Apprenticeship Agreement published by NJCBI

The following publications from HMSO:

Programme and Progress

Progress Charts for Housing Contracts

Site Records for Builders

The following Advisory Leaflets published by the Ministry of Public Building and Works:

No 7 *Concreting in Cold Weather*

No 8 *Bricklaying in Cold Weather*

No 13 *Site Costing for Builders*

No 18 *Powered Hand Tools—Electric Tools*

No 19 *Powered Hand Tools—Pneumatic Tools*

No 20 *Powered Hand Tools—Maintenance and Safety Precautions*

No 22 *Care of Small Plant and Hand Tools*

No 33 *Care of Builders' Machines*

No 36 *Metal Scaffolding*

No 40 *Weather and the Builder*

No 48 *Setting out on a Site*

No 54 *Woodworking Machinery for Builders*

No 59 *Electricity on Building Sites*

No 62 *Maintaining Exposed Woodwork*

No 63 *Fire Risks on Building Sites*

No 67 *Building without Accidents*

No 71 *Site Lighting*

No 72 *Noise Control on Building Sites*

No 74 *Protective Screens and Enclosures*

Also the following:

British Standard BS 4484, *Measuring Instruments for Constructional Works*, Part 1

BS Code of Practice, CP 97 *Metal Scaffolding*, Part 2 and *Suspended Scaffolds* (1970)

The Construction (General Provisions) Regulations, S1, 1580 (1961)

Index

factory, 88
public health, 88
Instant conversion, metric, 137
Interim Certificates, 196
Intermediate sight, 136
Inverted staff readings, 135

Job, break down, 42
Joint Council, history, 214, 215
purpose and duties, 216
structure, 216

Labour, costs, 38
records, 170
Ladders, 92, 99
Leaders, 20
Ledgers, 96, 97, 100
Levelling, 123, 124, 125
pegs, 123
terms, 135, 136
Levelling staffs, types, 134
markings, 134, 135
Line level, 123
Line of sight, 126, 132
Local Authority Notices, 165, 166

Machines, records, 65
Manager, general, 86
contracts, 86
departmental, 86
site, 87
the foreman as, 21
Management, the foreman's place, 20
Material, store ledger, 164
Materials, arrival, 58
bulky, 59
costing, 38
defective, 59
disposition, 57
fixed, 59, 60
handling, 59
layout, 58
ordering, 54
protection, 59, 60
records, 170, 171
return to stock, 165
stored, 164
waste, 34, 59
Measurement, building work, 195
for interim certificate, 196
Measuring, for variations, 199
Meetings, site, 168-70
Method study, 77, 79
Ministry of Environment, 89

Modification, 43

Negotiation, 214
Notice, of completion, 167
of commencement, 167
giving of, 167, 168
intention to build, 165, 167
Notices, local authority, 165, 166
official, 104, 105
NFBTE, 203, 204
objectives of, 204
safety signs, 231
NFBTO, 212, 213
NHBRC, 205, 206
guarantee, 206
NJAB, 226
NJATC, 226
NJCBI, 214

Observations, detailed, 78
random, 78
Office requirements, 149, 150
Optical square, 111, 112, 113
Order books, 157, 158, 159
Ordering materials, 54, 157
Ordnance Datum, 136, 137, 138
Organisation, good, 39
of firm, 84
repairs, 142
Overheads, 29
Overtime, 40, 143

Painters, Trade Union history, 212
Payment methods, 70
Plans, weekly, 47
deposit of, 167, 168
Planning, detailed, 44
engineer, 86
labour and materials, 56
preparation, 42
short term, 45
Plant, 55, 63
foreman's responsibility, 61
maintenance, 64
operation and maintenance, 61
records, 64, 65, 172
siting, 60
Precautions, safeguarding properties, 144
Preliminaries, 197
Price-selling, 29
Prime Cost, 29, 197
Profile boards, 122
Programme, 49
chart, 51
planning, 41